PACIFIC CHARTER

HALLETT ABEND

PACIFIC CHARTER

OUR DESTINY IN ASIA

Essay Index Reprint Series

BOOKS FOR LIBRARIES PRESS
FREEPORT, NEW YORK

First Published 1943
Reprinted 1972

Library of Congress Cataloging in Publication Data

Abend, Hallett Edward, 1884-1955.
  Pacific charter.

  (Essay index reprint series)
  Reprint of the 1943 ed.
  1. Reconstruction (1939-1951)--Asia.
2. Reconstruction (1939-1951)--Oceanica. I. Title.
D829.A75A2 1972   940.53'1   72-4478
ISBN 0-8369-2932-2   10-17-74

PRINTED IN THE UNITED STATES OF AMERICA

This Is
for
Salie

PACIFIC CHARTER

Contents

Contents

CHAPTER I

A Plea for Prejudice

THIS is a frank plea in favor of prejudice. The dictionaries say that a prejudice is an aversion, a partial decision formed in advance of argument or evidence; that it is grounded often upon feeling, fancy, or associations; and a prejudice, the definitions say, is always unfavorable unless the contrary is expressly stated.

The American people began with a violent prejudice against Japan in 1931 and 1932 when the Japanese Army started the conquest of Manchuria and when they bombed defenseless Shanghai. They entertained a prejudice against Hitler and his ways and works from 1933 onward. These prejudices were natural aversions, based upon instinctive feelings that the things the Japanese and Nazis were doing were inherently wrong and even vicious.

Through the years, however, our people and our Government did not bar argument or evidence. We listened to both to the point of nausea, but finally our prejudices, or hostile prejudgments, of Japanism and Nazism became settled convictions. These prejudices were founded, as we now devoutly believe, upon an instinctive recoil from wrong and evil, and as such should not now be condemned. We knew it was wrong for Japan to filch the Manchurian provinces from China, and there was almost unanimous Congressional and public approval when our Government announced that it would never recognize territorial changes effected by the use of force. We knew that peace became imperiled when Hitler began breaking treaties and rearming Germany.

For a decade we listened to Japanese arguments in defense of their policies. For nine years we listened to Nazi Germany's justifications. We did not rush into war without weighing arguments and evidence for long, tense years. During those years our prejudgments or prejudices were ever more and more justified, and they hardened into such convictions and policies that finally Japan and Germany attacked us. They attacked because they knew our convictions had become so firm that they could never achieve their ends without first destroying us.

Our prejudices, we now believe, were more than justified by acts and facts of later development, and our determination to total victory is based upon the deep belief that our prejudices were soundly based upon an instinctive spiritual rejection of evil—evil which threatened not only our own safety and existence but the freedoms and decencies of men and women everywhere in the world.

This book is based upon prejudice and is written in the belief that there should be no attempt at neutrality by those who write for the American public about this war against the aggressor nations. There will be here little discussion of Hitler or Nazism or Fascism, because the author has never lived in Europe and knows it only as a vacationing traveler may know lands through which he journeys in some haste and upon pleasure bent. This will be a book about the Far East and the problems of the Far Pacific, because the author lived in the Orient for nearly fifteen years, during all of which time he was busy reporting facts, watching the development of national policies and ambitions, and traveling widely in order to see the problems of East Asia in their various interrelations, instead of merely as they would appear to a resident who knew only China, or only Japan, or only the Philippine Islands.

The United States has been prejudiced against Japan and Germany and Italy since those countries forsook the ways of fair dealing and international honor. And now, as a nation, and with near unanimity as a people, we have pledged our resources, our utmost efforts, and our whole future to an endeavor to wipe out of the world the things which the aggressor nations represent. We have declared that, so long as the principles of Japanism, Nazism, and

Fascism continue, this world will not be a fit place for ourselves or for our children to live in.

Are these pledges and declarations, then, only propaganda and oratory, or do we mean what we say? If we are in deadly earnest in our declarations, then what place in today's grim scheme of things have pleas for an aloof neutrality of mind?

Of course we are prejudiced, and it is right that we should be so, for the events of many years have shown that our prejudgment of the acts and policies of the aggressor nations was soundly based. It took us years to make up our minds that the issues over which first China and then Britain and France and the other democracies were fighting were worth making war about. Now that we are in the war, it is time to abandon questionings and makeshifts and pretenses that we are unbiased. Of course we are biased—violently so —and this is as it should be, once we have decided that we face an evil so great that we must risk our very existence to help eradicate it from the world.

Since the persons who read these lines presumably intend to continue reading several tens of thousands of words of following exposition and argument, they are entitled to know when and why I first became prejudiced against Japanese policy in the Far East, and what the major events were which solidified my prejudgment against Japan into a settled conviction that an American-Japanese war was inevitable.

From the time when I first went to the Far East, early in 1926, until the close of 1931, I greatly admired Japan and the Japanese people. The disorders and extortions and cruelties in China during the years of civil war seemed to me appalling and unjustified, and I found the mendacity of much of the Soviet-inspired anti-imperialist Chinese propaganda offensive.

Peiping was my home and working headquarters during my first three years in the Far East, and during most of that time the Chinese provinces north of the Yangtze River were ruled by various satraps who shamefully oppressed and enslaved millions of their helpless countrymen. By contrast with the misery and misgovernment which then existed in Chihli and Shantung provinces, the way law and order were maintained in the Japanese-controlled South Manchuria Railway zone seemed praiseworthy, as indeed it was.

The Japanese had rights in Manchuria: rights gained by fighting a desperate war against Czarist Russia, rights obtained by treaty with China, and some "rights" obtained by bribery and scandalous intimidation. They also suffered wrongs in Manchuria. The Chinese managed to break or evade their proper and improper obligations to Japan. It is an old story now, a story of wrongs by both sides, but certainly Japan was goaded into taking punitive military action. We sent Pershing and a sizable army into Mexico on far less provocation than Japan initially acted upon in Manchuria. But Pershing's army came home, and we did not set up a puppet government in Mexico as Japan has done in Manchuria.

In the autumn and early winter of 1931, after the so-called "Mukden incident" of September 18 of that year, success went to the heads of the Japanese military in Manchuria, and they began to show openly the duplicity, callousness, and disregard for honor and good faith which have characterized their fabulously successful career ever since.

It is difficult to believe evil of those whom one has learned to admire and respect. I recall vividly the shock, late in October of 1931, with which I realized that although the Japanese kept continuing to assure Washington and London and Geneva that their armies would "retire into the Railway Zone as soon as order is restored," actually they had no intention of ever so retiring, but planned the conquest of all of Manchuria.

Then came the cynical affair of Chinchow.

One wintry day in 1931 the foreign correspondents at Mukden were excited by the transit southward, toward China proper and the Great Wall, of trainload after trainload of Japanese troops and supplies. The trains went through at twenty-minute intervals, and a military movement of the first magnitude was obviously being launched. There could be only one objective, the little walled city of Chinchow on the Peiping-Mukden Railway near the Great Wall. Chinchow was then the last administrative and military center in the hands of the Chinese Government in all of Manchuria. If it fell to the Japanese, Tientsin and Peiping would be immediately imperiled.

At this juncture our then Secretary of State, Mr. Stimson, sent so sharp a note to Tokyo that the militarists became alarmed, and the trainloads of troops and supplies were hauled back to Mukden without Chinchow's being assaulted. In fact, Tokyo officially assured the American Government that the Japanese armies would never attempt the capture of Chinchow or an approach to the Great Wall.

By that time my faith in the assurances of any Japanese was at zero. I went to General Honjo, who commanded all the Japanese forces in Manchuria, and asked him openly when he intended to capture Chinchow. He smiled, made no denial of intention, and asked why I wanted the information. I explained that I had been away from my home and office in Shanghai for nearly three months, that I wanted to straighten out many business affairs there, and hoped to spend Christmas in Shanghai. General Honjo made no direct reply, but called an orderly and told him to summon Major Watari, then the foreign-press contact man at Japanese Army headquarters. When the major appeared, General Honjo gave him the following instructions:

"Major, Abend wishes to go to Shanghai for Christmas, but also wishes to be present for the capture of Chinchow. See that he is warned in plenty of time to get back here. Note his address, and cable him the one word 'Come' when the time is ripe."

Here was the commander in chief of all the Japanese land forces on the Asiatic mainland arranging for an American newspaper correspondent to be present at the capture of a Chinese city which the Tokyo Government was assuring the American Government Japan would never attack!

Major Watari carried out instructions, but somehow the affair was bungled. On December 26 he cabled to me, "Come." I engaged passage on a steamer sailing from Shanghai on the twenty-seventh, which would have landed me at Dairen on the twenty-ninth. But five hours later, on the twenty-sixth, came another cable from Watari saying, "Wait a while." Then on the twenty-ninth came a third cable reading, "Come now, hurry!" I hurried, but could not reach Dairen until January 1, and Chinchow, several hundred miles away, was captured by the Japanese by assault in the morning hours of New Year's Day, 1932.

In that same month, on January 28, in Shanghai, my good opinion of the Japanese received a further setback.

Tension at Shanghai had become so extreme that I had left the Manchurian news field and returned to the great Chinese seaport on the twenty-fifth of the month. The Japanese were making demands having to do with local order and safety, the cessation of anti-Japanese movements, and Chinese preparations for possible hostilities.

On the afternoon of the twenty-eighth I enjoyed cocktails with Admiral Shiozawa in his private quarters on his flagship, and he told me without reserve that at eleven o'clock that night Japanese marines would advance into and take over the Chinese section of Shanghai known as Chapei. I asked the reason, and recalled to him that earlier in the afternoon the Chinese authorities had accepted all the Japanese demands and had formally signed the agreement upon which Japan insisted. The admiral's explanation was that the Chinese police, in a panic, had fled from Chapei, where about 6,000 Japanese civilians lived in the midst of 600,000 Chinese. Japanese marines, he said, would be sent in to "preserve order." When I got ashore I immediately telephoned to the American consul general, then Edwin S. Cunningham.

"But, Abend, you must be wrong," he protested. "Please do not cable such alarming news to the United States. The Japanese consul general himself called not more than half an hour ago to assure me that the tension is ended, now that the Chinese have accepted the Japanese demands."

But Admiral Shiozawa's marines did advance into Chapei at eleven o'clock that night. The Chinese resisted, as they were sure to do, and entirely within their rights to do. The fighting lasted into early March and cost the lives of about 35,000 uniformed and civilian Chinese and Japanese.

These incidents developed anti-Japanese prejudice. Well, and why not?

The prejudice became a settled conviction of the evil of Japanese policy and methods in the summer of 1937, when it became evident that Japan was going to attack in North

China. This attack was cold-bloodedly planned, and was not designed to redress any grievance, but was made solely because China's unification and strength were developing so soundly and so rapidly that Japan feared to wait longer. She felt she had to strike then, or forever abandon her schemes for the domination of East Asia. The fact that she misjudged China's strength and had waited too long is now history.

These events, particularly, and many others of a similar nature changed me from a friendly admirer of Japan into a questioning critic and finally into a condemning judge. My criticism and my judgment eventually goaded the Japanese into retaliatory measures. They sent hired thugs to ransack my apartment, beat and kick me, and steal my papers. Later they made attempts at assassination, and finally drove me from my home and from the field in which I had lived and worked for nearly fifteen years.

It was not their treatment of me as an individual which prejudiced me against the Japanese. My first prejudice was all in their favor. It was their methods and conquests on the Asiatic mainland which changed that first feeling into an adverse prejudice and finally into a settled conviction. And it was the written expression of this conviction which led them to retaliate with violence.

It must be shocking for Americans who have never been to the Orient to sit down with a map and trace the boundaries of the vast empire which the Japanese have conquered, to add up the statistics of the square miles of territories they have overrun and the totals of the subject people they now rule and exploit. It is doubly shocking to anyone who has lived in the Far East for fifteen years, and knows most of the cities Japan has ruined as well as he knew his home town as a boy.

Harbin in the far north, where the winter days are short and the mercury sinks to more than 40 below zero. Singapore, almost on the Equator, where there are no differing seasons and almost no difference the year through in the length of days and nights. Harbin and the frozen Sungari River, with the snows upon its banks glittering under the banners of the northern lights. Singapore, with its blue sea and the golf course where the player gets a free lift from any depression made by the trampling of a jungle beast.

Mukden and other Manchurian cities, where only the Japanese women wear fine furs and splendid silks, and the Chinese women shiver in ragged cottons. Peiping the beautiful, where nearly 100,000 Japanese troops are regularly quartered, and where the once quiet streets and huttings now blaze with neon lights in front of beer halls and Korean red-light houses and opium dives, in front of which red-faced, drunken Japanese soldiers kick and cuff the Chinese civilians and ricksha coolies at will.

Shameen, where the wild doves coo in the banyan trees at dawn; and Hongkong, where The Peak used to glitter at night and reflect its beauty in the black water of the harbor.

Manila, where a magnificent experiment in educating a whole people for self-government has almost been brought to fruition; Manila, now a blasted and fire-blackened ruin, with darkened and mournful Corregidor crouching across the harbor.

Shanghai and Canton, and Batavia and Rangoon. Penang and Bali, and Hanoi and Tsingtao. I have known them all well, and I have seen most of them bombed and shelled and brought to pestilence and hunger and despair by the Japanese invaders.

My "prejudice" against Japan is not based on the fact that my American and European friends have had to pack in haste and flee ignominiously before the Japanese attackers. My "prejudice" is based on the fact that I have seen how Japan rules and oppresses the Koreans, the Manchurians, and the Chinese in the lands she has overrun. Certainly she is no more generous with the Filipinos, the Malays, or the peoples of Java. Time will heal the grief of those who survive the millions who have been killed. Cities can and will be rebuilt. But while Japan rules and exploits the peoples she has conquered (and they number one fifth of all the inhabitants of the globe), education and all the freedoms will be suppressed, and the lash of the conqueror will be laid hard upon all the backs which are not bowed in obedience to the arrogant sons of Nippon.

This evil thing which is Japanism has finally forced the sons of America into a kind of war not understood here, but it is well that it should be understood so that our "prejudice" against Japanism shall not become dulled under preachments favoring a soft peace.

During more than five years of this same war more than 1,500,000 Chinese uniformed men have been killed, and American soldiers must now die the same kinds of death. On the bleak winter plains of Manchuria I have seen great mounds of Chinese dead left unburied, to be worried and gnawed into heaps of bones by the wolves and wild dogs.

In Tientsin, in the summer of 1937, I watched the Japanese use boat hooks and pikes to tumble hundreds and hundreds of the stripped bodies of Chinese soldiers into the river. It is a tidal river. The corpses first sank and then came to the surface. With the ebbing tide they would float a few miles downstream; with the flood they would sweep up past the city again. And this went on for days in the heat of July.

In Shanghai, in August and September of that same year, the smoke of heaps of burning bodies blew over the International Settlement in choking, nauseating clouds night after night.

At Manila and Hongkong and in all tropical East Asia, the heat and the humidity force the burial of the dead within twenty-four hours after death. But there was little time to bury our soldier, sailor, and Marine dead at Bataan.

At Shanghai I have seen a single bomb kill 600 people and wound and cripple 400 more. When a 750-pound bomb lands in a busy street, all life and movement seems to be halted for a period of three or four minutes. Nothing stirs except the eddying dust, drifting smoke, and the occasional crumbling of jarred masonry. The air is filled with the smell of hot blood and choking gas. Then, after what seems an eternity of suspended motion and silence, the wounded begin to moan or scream and struggle to their hands and knees and crawl about aimlessly. Then come the clang and wailing sirens of ambulances and fire-fighting apparatus, and life begins once more.

I have a prejudice against these things. I have a deep prejudice against nations which glorify aggression and slaughter. I have a conviction that they must first be disarmed and made powerless to resume their evil ways, and a conviction that then they must be re-educated in honor and in decency and in a new respect for the rights of fellow men and weaker nations.

I make again my frank plea in favor of prejudice. I urge the American people to keep burningly alive their prejudices against Japanism and Nazism and Fascism, and their determination to wipe these evils from the earth.

CHAPTER II

Wanted: Blueprints for Peace

SELF-APPOINTED ENEMIES have attacked the United States and forced us into total war. Our Government has announced, and our President has reiterated, that we intend to wage this war through to a total victory. So far, so good.

But after we win a total victory, then what? Should we not formulate in detail the things for which we are fighting? Do we wish to struggle through another peace conference like that held at Versailles, where conspiracy and intrigue, selfishness and half-baked doctrinaires pulled wires and brought pressures for selfish ends? Why wage a total war and insist upon a total victory unless we intend to impose a total peace? We are committed, together with thirty other nations, to defeat Nazism, Japanism, and Fascism. We owe it to ourselves, we thirty-two champions of President Roosevelt's "four freedoms," to let not only our enemies but the oppressed peoples of the world, and the few remaining neutrals, know what kind of world is planned after the total victory is won.

Another peace arrangement based upon bargain and barter will probably result in the obliteration of civilization as we now know it. Inspiring generalizations will not suffice this time as they did in 1917–18. During the first World War we fired the imaginations of the peoples of Europe by promising "self-determination," and then acquiesced in trading millions of them into irredentas where they were newly oppressed.

Twenty-five years ago we began participation in a gigantic struggle to "make the world safe for democracy" and to win "the war to end all wars." We won, but democracy and the democratic way of life have been losing ground for a dozen years. Instead of our victory ending war, conflict has succeeded conflict, wanton aggressions have become manifold, and now we are again engaged in a war—a war so terrible that it makes the human and economic cost of the 1914-18 struggle seem picayune by comparison.

The attitude and efforts of the thirty-two United Nations are based on the conviction that the peoples of Germany, Japan, and Italy have supported leaders and policies inimical to human freedom, and that these leaders must be punished and these policies must be abandoned. What then is to be our plan?

In 1918 the Kaiser abdicated and scurried to Holland.

Kings and princes and regents fled from their palaces and capitals in such numbers and in such haste that other less spectacular abdications merited only four- or five-line items in the newspapers. When we have won the promised total victory in this war, are the leaders of Nazism, Japanism, and Fascism to be permitted to slip away to the safety of neutral soil while our representatives sit down and bargain and haggle with their successors over what the victory of the United Nations really is to imply?

Our men are not dying on the four quarters of the globe to bring about another repetition of the Versailles Conference. The peoples of the thirty-two United Nations are not ready to undergo deprivations and hardships hitherto unknown in modern times, and then leave the vast issues of the future to be haggled over in secret by silk-hatted dignitaries intent upon selfish settlements designed to bring about a division of spoils or to perpetuate or re-establish imperialisms or national monopolies which will serve only to bring about more terrible wars in the future.

Work should be begun at once on blueprints for peace. The United Nations should define as explicitly as possible what they are fighting for. These blueprints need be no more final as to some details than are the blueprints for building a house. Homeowners, architects, and contractors know how such blueprints are nearly always changed while work is under way—a partition knocked out here, a new window cut there.

But the United Nations have not as yet even decided upon the dimensions of the foundations, how deep they are to be laid, or even the thickness and strength of the foundation walls. Deciding these fundamental questions and letting the decisions be made known to the world will admit of no more delay. Changes in the blueprints for the superstructure can and will be made as the war drags on, as new nations take sides, as conditions brought about in various regions by the conflict alter regional prospects and needs.

One objection to publicizing the proposed peace terms is that this will make our enemies fight on with renewed and desperate determination, but this can be easily overruled. The leaders of Nazism, Japanism, and Fascism know that they have all to gain or all to lose, and they will fight on and on so long as their peoples support them.

After all, nothing could spur the leaders of the Axis powers to more serious and sustained resistance than the White House announcement, concurred in by London, to the effect that the guilty chiefs of all enemy countries will be tried and punished for their crimes after the United Nations win a smashing victory in the war.

The candid enunciation of peace terms of fundamental justice might win war-wearied peoples of the enemy countries to withholding support from their leaders, and it is certain that the announcement of peace terms, if they are sound and right, would not only hearten our hard-pressed allies, but spur subject peoples and those who have been conquered by our foes to a vast acceleration of guerrilla activities and sabotage damaging to the strength of our foes.

The peoples now subject to Japan's tyranny have no definite idea of what the future is to hold for them after Japan has been defeated, therefore as yet they have no specific incentive for rallying to our cause. This continued neglect to arouse the support of several hundred million Asiatics is a persistent weakness which suggests that there is serious lack of unity in the war aims of the leaders of the United Nations.

Consider China, Korea, and Manchuria. China joined the Allies during the first World War, but the Versailles Treaty betrayed China and gave Japan a foothold in Shantung.

During the first World War the Korean people thought that "self-determination" was a promise to them of freedom from the Japanese yoke. They were bitterly disappointed, and considered themselves betrayed. Today Korea should be definitely promised freedom and eventual self-rule.

China should be pledged the righting of all the wrongs she has suffered at the hands of Japan during the last half-century.

Manchuria should be promised that the Japanese tyranny there will be brought to an end.

There are about 24,000,000 Koreans, 35,000,000 Manchurians, and 120,000,000 Chinese in the area now dominated by the Japanese Army. If these people, nearly 180,-

000,000 collectively, knew what a United Nations victory would mean to them in the way of freedom and security, their accelerated active help to our cause would keep three or four Japanese divisions well occupied.

Tokyo today rules 400,000,000 human beings. Here, in detail, are the incredible figures:

In Japan itself	70,000,000
In Korea	24,000,000
In Manchuria	35,000,000
In occupied China	120,000,000
In the Philippines	16,000,000
In Formosa and other islands	5,000,000
In French Indo-China	25,000,000
In Siam	14,000,000
In Malaya	5,000,000
In Burma	16,000,000
In Netherlands East Indies	70,000,000
Total	400,000,000

The Philippines have been definitely promised not only the restoration of freedom, but independence. China has been promised justice—but nothing specific. But the Manchurians, the Koreans, the Formosans, the Cambodians and Annamites of Indo-China, the Siamese, the Malayans, the Burmese, and the millions of the East Indies have no notion of what a United Nations victory will mean to them. They should be told.

And the 70,000,000 people of Japan should be told what the future holds for them. They probably fear that defeat will bring them poverty, hunger, oppression, and crushing and vengeful indemnities. They should be assured to the contrary.

Japan's hold upon vast areas stretching from near the Arctic Circle in the north to far south of the Equator in the East Indies is being tightened every day. Roughly 195,000,-000 people in occupied China, Korea, Manchuria, and the Philippines have high hopes of more or less definite freedoms after the United Nations defeat Japan, but the 135,000,000 people of the East Indies, Malaya, Burma, Siam, Indo-China, and Formosa have been assured of nothing more definite than the phrases in the Atlantic Charter about recognizing the rights of all peoples to choose their own form of government. And the people of Japan have nothing but dread of a future of unspecified humiliation and hardship in case their own present harsh taskmasters are defeated.

The theory is often proffered, and supported by many a fallacy, that, once Germany has been defeated, Japan will have to fold up her tents and go home. But those who support this thesis seem never to have considered the strong probability that Japan did not attack the democracies in compliance to pleas or orders from Berlin, but that she acted with calculated craft and entirely in her own self-interest. It is more than probable that Japan's simultaneous

attack upon American, British, and Netherlands outposts in
the Far Pacific was a move taken in the nature of insurance
against a possible German defeat. Japan doubtless does not
expect Germany to be beaten, but neither does the man who
takes out fire insurance expect his home to burn down.

As late as December 6 of 1941 Japan's strategic position in East Asia was vulnerable and dangerous, and her
reserves of fuel oil and gasoline were critically low. On that
date her farthest advance southward was French Indo-
China, and she was perilously encircled by potential
enemies. We held the Philippines to the east of Indo-China,
the Dutch held the Indies to the south, Britain was en-
trenched in Singapore, Malaya, and Burma to the south and
west, and China was to the northwest. Thus precariously
placed, Japan was forced by her own peril to strike southward with all the strength she could muster. She could not
risk remaining inactive where she was, for, had Hitler met
defeat while that strategic situation continued unchanged
in the Far Pacific, Japan would have been hopelessly placed.
Therefore she struck southward—hard. She succeeded
rapidly and completely, and today is so strongly situated in
and adjacent to southeast Asia that she need not be too
greatly concerned over Germany's ultimate fate. If she is
left in undisturbed possession of her newly conquered
territories for twelve or eighteen months more her power
may well double.

Just as Germany is reorganizing the industrial and economic life of much of Europe so that almost all of that continent is working for the Third Reich, so is Japan reorganizing the occupied provinces of China and all the lands and archipelagos southward to work for the enhancement, wealth, and power of the Empire. Japan is doing more than imposing a harsh military rule upon the native peoples in the lands she has conquered. She is working them hard. She is not content with merely the military occupation of key cities, railways, harbors, and airdromes. From occupied China she is obtaining vast quantities of coal and iron and various foods. From Indo-China and Siam she obtains more rice than she needs for her armies abroad and to make up the lag in home production due to the draining of peasants into her military services and armament factories.

At Penang the British did not destroy the priceless tin smelter. That great plant now works day and night, and the tin mines of Malaya and the East Indies produce ample ore. There was no time for the defeated armies and peoples to hack down even a third of the rubber trees on the plantations of Malaya and Java and Sumatra. Japan today actually has more rubber than she knows what to do with. In the Philippines she is reopening the gold and iron and chromite mines. Her transport ships do not return homeward empty from the Philippines and Java—they carry profitable cargoes of sugar, for one thing, and abundant supplies of quinine which help her armies fight off malaria.

A short news dispatch published in this country on May 14, 1942, gave a hint of what is going on. It told of the torpedoing and sinking of one of the largest Japanese passenger ships in the South China Sea, and detailed that the 540 survivors were made up of financial, industrial, and economic leaders and chemical experts and engineers who were southbound when their vessel was destroyed.

All over the conquered lands the great Japanese banks and shipping and insurance companies are opening large branches. Huge properties of all kinds are being bought up for next to nothing. In some cases real money is used, but in general these acquisitions are plain thefts, for the so-called money paid over is the totally unsecured Japanese military yen. This currency has no specie, security, or legal backing of any kind. It comes from the Army's printing presses and is forced upon the people of the occupied lands at the point of the bayonet. Japan already utterly dominates the finance, trade, agriculture, industry, and politics over rich lands so populous that their combined inhabitants number nearly three times the population of the United States.

Early in 1942 the oil fields of Borneo, Sumatra, and Burma began pouring out wealth and essential fuels for the benefit of the Japanese. To be sure, the Dutch and British destroyed their wells and pipe lines and refineries, but Japan has long known that they intended this destruction. Before she attacked Pearl Harbor her warehouses and docks were well crammed with drilling rigs, pipe, refinery machinery.

And she has been building tankers at a prodigious rate for the last four years.

The sordid drama of greed and legalized pillage enacted in the occupied portions of China since 1937 is being re-enacted today in the Philippines, the East Indies, Malaya, Indo-China, and Burma. Japan organized a bank without any paid-in capital in Peiping soon after the occupation, and then formed the North China Development Company with a nominal capital of 300,000,000 yen. In Shanghai she organized the Central China Development Company with 100,000,000 yen capital, and ordered Wang Ching-wei to set up a "Central Bank" at Nanking. The North China and Nanking banks then issued valueless paper money, and the Chinese were forced to accept it in exchange for sound currency. The development companies "bought" railways and power plants and docks and factories, giving this worthless currency or the equally worthless military yen in payment. Similar "development" companies and banks are being organized to absorb all the wealth of all the lands Japan has newly occupied or conquered.

Over all this immense area factories which are not producing goods essential to Japan's war effort or Japan's home needs are forced to close down by the simple expedient of cutting them off from the purchase of raw materials. In some cases essential machinery is being confiscated and removed to Japan or to Manchuria. In all the conquered lands all the railways, river and coastal shipping, air lines, and such ocean shipping as exists are now controlled and operated by Japanese—first for the convenience of the Japanese Army and Navy, and second for the profit of Japanese holding companies.

No one of the occupied countries is permitted to trade freely with any of the others. All trade must go through Japanese clearinghouses, and each transaction must have the approval of the military before it can be concluded. The military, in turn, charge outrageously large fees for "inspection services," but these fees do not enrich the treasury of the Japanese Empire. By common consent they enrich the Japanese military. There is no quarreling over the division of the spoils, for recognized "cuts" are automatically assigned to all concerned, from major generals down to corporals.

If Japan is to be permitted to continue unmolested the organization and looting of the lands she occupies, if she succeeds in entirely transforming their industries and production to the support of her war machine, her strength will increase prodigiously.

American and other United Nations military and naval leaders admit that Japan must be given no rest and must be permitted no sense of strategic security in the regions which she has overrun. It is equally important that she be also continuously harassed and distracted politically in the lands in which she is attempting to establish her infamous "New Order." The several hundred million people whom she now exploits and rules must be told specifically what they stand to gain from Japan's defeat. The will to active and passive resistance and to measures of non-co-operation must be stimulated and encouraged in every way.

This book is in no sense an attempt to outline blueprints for the peace. It is an exposition of the difficult problems which the makers of peace will have to face in the Orient, in Indonesia, and in regions adjacent to the Far East. It is a summary of what the peoples native to those regions want and should be assured that they will be given after the United Nations win the war.

Destiny is forcing upon the United States the role of arbiter of the future of hundreds of millions of human beings. They look to us for a belated opportunity for deliverance from political and economic servitudes of varying degrees of harshness or benevolence. They expect the United States to act as their liberator, their champion, and their protector in the days when they grope their way to self-respecting liberty and self-government.

It has become evident since Pearl Harbor that we and the Chinese must do most of the fighting in order to assure the defeat of Japan, unless Soviet Russia joins in the struggle later. And circumstances not of our making nor of our wishing will also force us to do most of the work of securing a just peace in the Far East. The peoples of the Orient look to us to do more than drive out their present Japanese oppressors. They are also confident that we will win the war so decisively that they will not again be in peril of aggression or conquest by Japan.

But they look to us for more than that. They believe that we will not connive at restoring political, social, or economic controls which Japan struck off by the use of force.

Obviously now is the time to obtain unbreakable pledges of freedom and justice for the hundreds of millions of people of Asia and the islands of the South Seas. All of our active allies are urgently in need of our assistance, our war supplies, our credits, our food, and our military re-enforcements. Those of them which have maintained imperialist holds upon subject peoples will, under the stress of fighting for survival, agree more readily now to justice for the yellow men and the brown than they would after the victory has been won.

When the fighting stops, all nations will be impoverished —we less than any of the others. Those with colonies will then want to renew their old dominations over subject peoples. They will want to exploit their former possessions in order to regain their own solvency and prosperity as soon as possible. If we wait until after the victory has been won, if we delay until a peace conference is called, there will certainly develop strains and stresses and intrigues and combinations designed to force the United States to agree to compromises that will make the peoples of the Orient feel that we have betrayed them and disappointed their high hopes in our sincerity of fighting for the eight points set forth in the Atlantic Charter and for the "four freedoms" enunciated by President Roosevelt—freedom of speech and expression, freedom of religious worship, freedom from want, and freedom from fear, "everywhere in the world."

Here are statements taken from addresses or state papers by President Roosevelt between midsummer of 1941 and midsummer of 1942 which have made the peoples of the Far East believe that this nation will not shirk the role of liberator in their part of the world:

The essence of our struggle is that men shall be free.

There must be no place in the postwar world for special privilege, either for individuals or nations.

This duty we owe . . . is to make the world a place where freedom can live and grow into the ages.

We are fighting today for security, for progress, and for peace, not only for one generation but for all generations. We are fighting to cleanse the world of ancient evils, ancient ills.

We are fighting, as our fathers have fought, to uphold the doctrine that all men are equal in the sight of God.

We of the United Nations are agreed on certain broad principles in the kind of peace we seek . . . disarmament of aggressors, self-determination of nations and peoples.

Those are high aims, nobly phrased. But the world heard similar aims expressed in stirring words by President Wilson a quarter of a century ago.

The Roosevelt-Churchill statement of August 14, 1941, called the Atlantic Charter, is more specific on many points.

Here are some of the pledged aims of the British Empire and the United States—aims which must necessarily apply to the Pacific area, too, even though they were formulated on shipboard on the Atlantic during those historic meetings at sea of the leaders of the great democracies.

They desire to see no territorial changes that do not accord with the freely expressed wishes of the peoples concerned;

They respect the right of all peoples to choose the form of government under which they will live; and they wish to see sovereign rights and self-government restored to those who have been forcibly deprived of them;

They will endeavor, with due respect for their existing obligations, to further the enjoyment by all States, great or small, victor or vanquished, of access, on equal terms, to the trade and to the raw materials of the world which are needed for their economic prosperity.

The implication of these paragraphs to Norway is plain and self-evident. The Belgians and the Poles and Dutch and other conquered European peoples know what they mean. But what do they mean to the millions of inhabitants of French Indo-China, who have long been misgoverned and greedily exploited? What will they mean to the Burmese, who assisted the Japanese invaders? What will they mean to the 70,000,000 natives of the Netherlands East Indies? How are these promises interpreted in Siam and in Malaya? And, above all, what do these pledges mean to China, to India, and to the people of Japan?

Trade, fiscal, and economic readjustments must necessarily wait for detailed arrangements until after victory is won, for the burdens of the world's debts and the measure of the world's hunger and poverty cannot be estimated in advance. But if individual blueprints for the proposed political and national status of the peoples of the Far East were announced as pledges by the United Nations, and if those blueprints promised justice and gave the peoples now oppressed by Japan definite hopes, aims, and aspirations, then the Orient's attitude toward this war would vitalize and change, and Japan's task of holding what she has won would become trebly difficult.

Destiny has forced upon the United States two magnificent roles. This nation is the acknowledged arsenal of the democracies, and the hopes of hundreds of millions of human beings have also made us the ideological leader and mouthpiece of the United Nations.

The second role, properly played, can do as much toward winning the war as scores of convoys of fighting men and planes and guns and tanks.

CHAPTER III

Clipping Japan's Claws

GRANTING EVENTUAL VICTORY to the United Nations (and this book is written on the conviction that the Axis group will suffer total defeat), it is a foregone conclusion that one of the terms of the armistice, not to be delayed for the final peace, will be the complete disarming of Japan. Quite aside from the fact that the Atlantic Charter declares flatly for the disarmament of aggressor nations, the American public will be satisfied with nothing less, and even if the United States did not insist on disarming Japan, then China would insist on it as the major condition attached to the end of hostilities.

For nearly half a century Japan has been using her armed forces to expand her territory at the expense of her neighbors on the Asiatic mainland and of their possessions in adjacent seas. This process must be halted, and steps must be taken to make it impossible for Japan ever to resume her career of loot and conquest.

Without counting the 2,400 mandated islands in the Pacific which Japan obtained after the first World War, she now owns or controls more than 763,000 square miles of territory. And yet half a century ago the area of the Japanese Empire was only a little more than 147,000 square miles. She warred with China in the '90s and thereby obtained the island of Formosa and the Pescadores. She warred with Russia in 1904-05 and obtained the southern half of Sakhalin Island. Soon after the conclusion of the Russo-Japanese War she annexed Korea, although having repeatedly given pledges to the nations of the world to respect the independence of that ancient kingdom. These three expansions together totaled 113,000 square miles. Then, a decade ago, she completed the conquest of Manchuria, adding another 504,000 square miles.

Not counting the Chinese territory occupied since that frightful "incident" of invasion and slaughter which was begun in July of 1937, and not counting the vast territories she has overrun since the attack on Pearl Harbor and the push southward, the Japanese Empire, including the puppet state of Manchukuo, is five times larger than it was less than fifty years ago.

This expansive greed cannot be checked merely by disarming Japan. Her military caste must be utterly discredited, her entire system of education must be remade, and her form of government must be changed, even though the Atlantic Charter incautiously declares for "the right of all peoples to choose the form of government under which they will live." That ill-advised declaration will also surely not apply to Germany, where it would mean the perpetuation of the Nazi administration if the German people were to choose to continue to live under the rule of Hitler's party.

Nothing could so utterly discredit Japan's militarists as to have their treacherous onslaught on the democracies result in deposing the ruling house of the Empire, which according to a mythological history has descended in an unbroken line from the Sun Goddess for more than 2,600 years. To depose Emperor Hirohito would not be to rob the Japanese people of a divinity. They do not worship him as a god. He is regarded rather as the incarnation of the race and the history of the race. He is considered to be responsible to his ancestors for what occurs during his reign, but the people would never consider holding him personally responsible for the acts or policies sponsored or ordered by his Cabinet or by his various ministers.

The dangers inherent in Japan's form of government are many. The Emperor theoretically "appoints" his Prime Minister, but actually he has no voice in the choice of the head of his Cabinet. The Prime Minister must always be a man acceptable to the Army and the Navy—otherwise either or both of those services refuses to select a War or

Navy Minister, and without those portfolios satisfactorily assigned, no Cabinet can function.

Hirohito, although theoretically an absolute ruler, does not even have the right to choose his own Minister of War or Minister of the Navy. The Minister of War is chosen by the ranking heads of the Army and must be an active lieutenant general or general, and the Minister of the Navy must be a vice-admiral or an admiral on the active list. These heads and official representatives of the fighting forces are not responsible to the Premier or to the Cabinet, nor were they responsible to the Parliament when that body still functioned in Japan. They have personal access, and are responsible only, to the Emperor. The Emperor, however, does not give the chiefs of his military services orders; he accepts their advice.

The perpetuation of this system of government after the war would without fail lead to the rearming of Japan and to a new war in the Far East, just as the perpetuation of the military caste in Germany led to the rearming of the Reich, even though after 1918 Germany had virtually no Navy and her Army was theoretically limited to a defense force of 100,000 men. Whatever coast-defense force against smuggling Japan is permitted to retain after she is defeated and whatever military police she is allowed to have to maintain internal order, care must be taken that the leaders are chosen from circles which have had no previous connection with either the Navy or Army.

Emperor Hirohito, although he is only five feet two inches in height, enacts very well the pompous role of the 124th Emperor of his line, the supposed lineal descendant of the Sun Goddess. He is ever mindful that he is the living head of the oldest ruling dynasty in the world, a dynasty which Japan's Cabinet solemnly proclaimed in 1936 as being "Timeless as Heaven and Earth." Japanese propagandists like to represent their Emperor as being above knowledge of or contact with the ugly phases of Japan's career of expansion and conquest. They would like to have the rest of the world believe that Hirohito lives in a godlike realm of detachment from the sins and horrors of the world of everyday mortals and that he is concerned with abstractions like communing with his "eternal line of ancestors," or meditating upon "Japan's manifest destiny" and the "divine mission of the overlordship of East Asia."

Actually Hirohito is a very human sort of person. He is the father of half a dozen children; he keeps a tight control over the jealousies and quarrels of his brothers, uncles, aunts, and many cousins; and he keeps a jealous and watchful eye on the imperial fortune and investments. Many banking and financial experts rate Hirohito as the richest individual in the world today, and "the divine mind" is not above concerning itself with stocks and bonds and dividends and monopolies.

The size of the Japanese imperial fortune is difficult to determine, for the Emperor invests widely through the great Japanese banking and development houses of Mitsui and Mitsubishi. He owns, by inheritance and purchase, nearly a one-half interest in the billion-yen South Manchuria Railway, and even before his armies began their conquests southward he had enormous interests in the Philippines, Siam, and French Indo-China. In the Philippines these imperial investments, cloaked under dummy American and Filipino agents, ranged from breweries to mahogany forests and from fish-canning plants to profitable mining enterprises. In Japan the Emperor owns most of the forest lands as well as enormous areas of rice fields, and the same is true in Korea and Formosa.

Emperor Hirohito, who has never yet punished, reprimanded, or degraded any of the many of his military leaders who have been personally responsible for the atrocities in China which have continuously shocked the civilized world for more than five years, knows all about those atrocities. His lack of disciplinary action against the men who have been responsible signifies at least his tacit approval of their policies of frightfulness. I know that Hirohito is not ignorant of the shocking and lustful brutality of war, as practiced by his armies. I know that he had personal knowledge of the worst of the details of the rape of Nanking within less than three weeks after his soldiers were guilty of unprintable offenses against human dignity and decency in that city in December of 1937.

Early in January of 1938, only a few weeks after the

rape of Nanking, there called at my apartment a high civilian Japanese official who had made a personal investigation of the atrocities which the Japanese Army committed in China's captured capital. He had just returned from making his report at Tokyo, and that day he told me things about the conduct of Nippon's soldiers which I had not heard from other sources and which were too horrible to set forth in print.

Few Japanese will ever discuss their Emperor with foreigners, probably because they sense that we all consider their myth about his descent from the Sun Goddess to be absurd. This day, however, my caller finally imparted to me a conception of Hirohito which was new and startling.

"Foreigners," he began, "cannot realize the fact that the position of our ruler is absolutely unique amongst all men living in the world. He is the one man on the earth who has everything he can wish for; he is above ambition and above desire."

Here was a new idea indeed. My caller went on to explain that the Emperor of Japan has greater power than anyone in the world, that his own conviction of his divine descent puts him in a unique position of aloofness toward all mortal men. Hirohito's wealth, he further explained, also contributes to his security, and the abject reverence with which his subjects regard him also helps to place him "above ambition and beyond desire." Then came the revelation of Hirohito's personal knowledge of the horrors of Nanking and of the ruthless rape of China.

"I was accorded the very rare honor of a summons to the palace and of more than two hours of private conversation with the Emperor," my caller continued. "When I entered the great hall of audience, he ordered all attendants to retire to the doors, beyond hearing. Then he had a pillow placed for me, and I spent two hours on my knees at his feet, while he bent over and had me whisper into his ear all that I knew about the events following the capture of Nanking. I kept back nothing, and he asked many searching questions.

"The secret interview lasted so long that gradually my feet and legs became temporarily paralyzed, and when he finally had learned all he wanted to know, the Emperor graciously permitted me to continue kneeling while he arose and left the room. Court attendants then raised me to my feet, and I was massaged and exercised until I was able to walk unassisted once more."

So of course Hirohito knows how his militarists behave. He must know, by this time, all and more about their conduct at Hongkong than Anthony Eden told the House of Commons. And he doubtless knows more about the treatment of Americans and Filipinos in Manila than the American public has yet been permitted to learn.

When the question of the punishment of the war guilty of Japan arises, the peacemakers will face a difficult problem.

The names of generals in command of cities where atrocities
have occurred are, of course, well known; but who, for
instance, was responsible for the sneak attack on Pearl
Harbor? Who planned in detail and who acquiesced in the
bold scheme for attacking the Philippines, Malaya, and the
Netherlands East Indies? The Prime Minister, the Ministers
of War and Navy, and the heads of their staffs are, of course,
primarily guilty. And Emperor Hirohito, too, must have
known that the future of his Empire and his people was
being risked that December 7 and 8. But what about the
Emperor's group of personal advisers who are known in
Japan as the Court or the Throne?

This group of high and responsible officials does not
represent any political party. The members are appointed
one at a time, when vacancies occur, by whoever is Prime
Minister at that particular period. They are not responsible
to the Government, to the Premier, or to the Cabinet, and
they hold office for life and cannot be removed except by
imperial dismissal. This powerful group consists of the
Lord Keeper of the Imperial Seals, the Minister of the
Imperial Household, the Grand Chamberlain, and the
Grand Master of Ceremonies.

The imprint of the Imperial Seal is necessary to signify
the Emperor's assent to all new laws and ordinances, and
the Lord Keeper not only has custody of this powerful
talisman but also presides at all meetings of Court Council-
lors. Palace administration and the vast imperial fortune

come under the supervision of the Minister of the Imperial Household. The whole palace staff is under the Grand Chamberlain. These men have enormous influence upon policy, and it is through them, or when they are present, that the Emperor is advised on the state of his realm by the Prime Minister and the heads of the fighting forces. How greatly, if at all, any one of them may influence Hirohito's decisions and policies is not known outside the little palace circle itself, but it is noteworthy that whenever the radicals of the Army try to intimidate Cabinets they always plan the assassination of one or more of this small group of imperial advisers.

Japan has no leader in a position comparable to that of Hitler or to that of Mussolini. Administration is conducted by group rule, with the military services heading the strongest and most ruthless and ambitious inner group. Emperor Hirohito reigns, but the heads of the Army and Navy, by controlling the Prime Minister and having the power of dissolution over the Cabinet, are the men who really rule. But in spite of this division of power, it is certain that Hirohito himself approved in writing the attacks on Pearl Harbor and Hongkong, the invasion of the Philippines, Siam, Indo-China, the East Indies, and Burma. Without his permission those naval and military moves would have been impossible, as would the long war against China, for one of the most closely guarded imperial powers is that under which no naval or military force may go beyond Japan's own borders without an imperial rescript signed by the Emperor.

Only once in Japan's history has this particular imperial prerogative been ignored or defied. That was in September of 1931 when Japanese armies crossed the Yalu River from Korea into Manchuria. The imperial rescript authorizing the use of Japanese armies on Chinese soil was signed four days later, and with some reluctance. At that time there was said to have been tension and disagreement between Hirohito and his military leaders, and the Emperor signed on the dotted line because he feared that if he ordered his armies to return home they might defy him.

The Manchurian venture succeeded beyond expectations, and Hirohito became convinced that aggression and expansion were wise policies. Since then he has never disagreed with any new plans for conquest. It is this certainty of Hirohito's approval, connivance, and guilt which will technically justify depriving him of his throne at the end of the war.

Japan's educational system must be changed as radically as the governmental system before there can be lasting peace in the Pacific. During the last decade the military have gained absolute direction of the policies of education, and the generation now approaching maturity has been nurtured upon hate of the white man, contempt for the Chinese, and the dangerous concept that the Japanese people have been chosen by the high gods to rule all of East

Asia, and probably, at a later date, the whole world. Arrogance, aggression, brutality, and slaughter have been glorified in the texts and illustrations of all schoolbooks used from the primary grades on and up through the universities. So long as the school children of a nation of 70,000,000 people are all taught that they are of a superior and divinely chosen race and that by mere virtue of their birth and blood they have the right to rule all lesser breeds, the temper of the people will make Japan a danger to the whole hemisphere.

Probably 90 per cent of the people of Japan have been successfully educated to believe that the greed of the white races has prevented the Empire from attaining its rightful place in the sun. The tale which Japanese propagandists have successfully spread in this country and in Europe—that Japan is unjustly one of the "have not" nations and is justified by its growing population in grabbing the territories of its neighbors in order to obtain room for migration and to have access to raw materials—has come to be devoutly believed by the Japanese people themselves.

Japanese propagandists plead eloquently that the population of their home islands has doubled since President Fillmore sent Commodore Perry to Japan in 1853. But they neglect to state that the production of food has more than doubled within that same period, and they never make clear the fact that although the individual landholdings of farmers are pitifully small (the average is nine tenths of an acre), nevertheless the 53 per cent of the population who work these small farms contrive to make Japan so nearly self-supporting in the matter of food that a starvation blockade could never be made effective.

Japan pleads that she has not enough coal, oil, or iron ore for her own needs and grows no cotton, and that therefore she must be permitted to overrun and annex lands which produce these basic necessities. The United States might as well try to justify filching parts of Java and Malaya because it has no tin and grows no rubber.

Japan has always had access to all the raw materials she needed. The truth of this is shown by her marvelous industrial expansion. Japanese-made goods were being taken to every port in the world by Japanese-owned and Japanese-built ships before Japan began the most recent phase of aggressive expansion. Forty-seven per cent of the people of Japan made their living by industry and foreign trade, and the Japanese scale of living was the highest in Asia, until their own militarists began impoverishing the country by building up the world's third largest navy and a standing army of more than 1,000,000 men.

Apologists for Japan, when she took Manchuria and later attacked China in 1937, pleaded that expanding population and increasing poverty had brought about an "explosion." And yet the Empire's own statistics testify to a continuous trend of growing wealth and better living standards. These statistics show that in 1935 Japan's foreign trade was the greatest in her history—almost exactly 100 per cent greater than it was in 1931. Except during the world-wide depression of a decade ago, Japan's trade has increased every year for four fifths of a century.

Japanese have never emigrated in important numbers to any of the territories which their Imperial Government has wrenched away from Japan's neighbors. They have owned Formosa for nearly half a century, but Japanese civilian inhabitants of that island number only about 260,000. Since they annexed Korea the population of that hapless country has increased from 11,000,000 to 24,000,000. There was obviously ample room in Korea, but at the taking of the last census Japanese civilians there numbered less than 250,-000. For more than a decade Japan has maintained a system of lavish subsidies for all of her subjects who would emigrate to free land in Manchuria, but the total is less than 750,000.

If, by pleading the necessity of owning lands which are the source of raw materials, Japan means raw materials essential to war industries, then the excuse is sound. But if her plea refers only to the raw materials necessary for industrial prosperity, her own economic history gives her the lie. Japan did not conquer or annex any cotton-growing areas, and yet she gained control of the cotton trade to such an extent that the British cotton mills closed down one by one, and Lancashire suffered terrific unemployment because Japanese goods undersold the British product, even in India.

After defeat the Japanese will not be barred from the

world's markets, nor will their scale of living be lowered as a result of being deprived of essential raw materials. Instead, their scale of living should rise rapidly when they are freed from the terrible burden of supporting gigantic Army and Navy establishments. As for the question of raw materials and markets, the Atlantic Charter makes this pledge of intention:

"They will endeavor, with due respect for their existing obligations, to further the enjoyment by all States, great or small, victor or vanquished, of access, on equal terms, to the trade and to the raw materials of the world which are needed for their economic prosperity."

CHAPTER IV

China and Japan

Certainly one of the basic conditions for an enduring peace, and one which should be announced without reservations at the earliest possible date, is the permanent eviction of Japan from all of the Asiatic mainland and from all the islands and bases east of Asia which she has acquired since 1894. An announcement of this kind, backed by the unanimous pledge of all the United Nations, except Soviet Russia, would rekindle the flame of hope for 330,000,-000 Asiatics, even though it would infuriate the 70,000,000 Japanese to whom the loss of all of their conquests will be a frightful humiliation.

Drastic as this amputation of vast territories and subject people will seem to the Japanese and to many other people as well, it will be a necessary piece of territorial surgery—necessary not only because it will doubtless be one of

China's minimum demands in the day of victory, but also as a measure of protection for ourselves. Unless the wrongs and territorial thefts and holdups of the last half-century are righted at the close of this war, we shall have to fight again before even another quarter of a century has gone by.

The future status of China is the basic subject of the war between the United States and Japan. All other differences could have been settled by negotiation and compromise; even the Japanese admitted that in the last days of the Nomura-Kurusu parleys with Secretary Hull, just before the attack on Pearl Harbor. Abstention from further aggression, equality of commercial activities, the evacuation of southern Indo-China—all these things Japan was ready to grant. But Japan refused to evacuate any part of occupied China—refused even to discuss proposals looking toward that end. The United States grimly refused even by implication to discuss whether China was to be left to Japanese control or conquest. Compromise was clearly impossible, and so the Japanese rained bombs on Pearl Harbor.

Now that we are in this war—totally in it—what do we most want after we have won? The answer is simple and clear: we want a resulting status which will give at least reasonable assurance that we shall not have to participate in a total war again, in any case during the reasonable expectation of life of all the sons and daughters of the United States now living. We ardently desire and urgently need at least a century of peace. Our men in uniform are not fighting for a breathing spell of a decade or two. The country wants peace for today and tomorrow, and for all the tomorrows of millions of children, yet unborn, who will be sired by our fighters when finally they return from overseas. No lesser result could justify what we are sacrificing today or what we shall have to sacrifice in unnumbered grim days to come.

The proposal that Japan must be deprived of all her territorial gains of the last half-century is based on the assumption that the Empire must be literally crushed in a military sense. If the defeat is not decisive, the essential aims of the United Nations will not be achieved.

For nearly fifty years Japan has been expanding by making war upon weaker and unprepared neighbors. The Japanese people do not know what the devastation of war means. Ruin must be brought to their cities and villages to teach them a lesson concerning what they have inflicted upon other peoples. The Japanese people must live with and daily look upon reminders that reckless conquest and loot bring a frightful retribution. Only by such stern measures can the United Nations permanently impair the prestige of the military caste in Japan. The Japanese people must, in the future, have no heart for bloody adventures which imperil the peace of the world.

The defeat of Japan must also involve the absolute crushing of her power to assume the role of the aggressor for at least the next twenty-five years. Thus far the Japanese

Empire has never known defeat in any of the wars it has fought in modern times, nor have the people known warfare on their own soil. Each war has brought victory, enrichment, elation, and an enhancement of the prestige of the military caste. This war must end in the bitter lesson that international banditry brings fearful punishments. The terrible patriots of Nippon must be forced to give up the fruits of fifty years of predatory policies, not as a measure of a punitive peace, but primarily as a deterrent against an early revival of greedy militarism and as the minimum of the overdue justice owed to long-suffering China and Korea.

After the piratical militarists have been discredited and disarmed it will take a generation for the Japanese people to recover from a fundamental trouble similar to that which afflicts the German people—an ingrained false belief in their own fancied superiority to other peoples and a conviction that the unique structure of their state and the antiquity of their dynasty entitle them to rule and exploit half of Asia.

A great deal of strange reasoning is being circulated in the United States these days, arguing that for our own safety we should favor a strong Japan after the war. The contention is set forth that if China is completely restored, from northern Manchuria to the island of Hainan, "we shall have set up in Asia the sort of thing we are attempting to destroy in Europe—a huge and powerful China with a power potential of 450,000,000 would be as great a menace to peace as a Hitler-dominated Europe." It is true that China will make a relatively quick recovery from the ravages of war if she is given adequate credits and other assistance by this country, and thus China will soon become a tremendous power potential—but there is a vast difference between a potential and an actuality.

It is inconceivable that any one of the United Nations, having participated actively in suppressing the aggressors, will in any measurable future wish to assume the role of an aggressor. China, with the threat of Japanese political and military aggression definitely removed, will have no incentive to militarism. In fact, China's leaders of today have looked far ahead to the days of peace, and do not plan to build or maintain any navy at all, except small vessels necessary to the prevention of piracy and smuggling on her long coast line. With the coming of peace, and with a disarmed Japan, there will be no threat to China's borders, and the Chinese Government will be glad to demobilize the millions of men who will be under arms as quickly as the economic and agricultural life of the nation can absorb them.

China's Foreign Minister, T. V. Soong, gave the best outline of what he termed "the broad objectives for which my country believes it is fighting" that has yet emanated from Chinese Government circles. Speaking at an alumni luncheon of Yale University, Dr. Soong said, in part:

The first is political freedom for Asia. The World War of 1914, while it did not succeed fully in liberating all the nations of Europe, scarcely even touched Asia. Modern inventions have annihilated distances and multiplied contacts between nations, and the world can no longer exist peaceably half free, half enslaved, any more than, as Lincoln said, a single nation can.

China is fighting for her independence; she aspires equally for the freedom of all Asiatic nations. There are, of course, here and there certain nations which may not be ready as yet for complete self-government, but that should not furnish the excuse for colonial exploitation; the United States in the Philippines has furnished a notable example of disinterested temporary guardianship.

Our second objective is economic justice. Political and economic justice go together; without the one the other cannot flourish. Asia is tired of being regarded only in terms of markets and concessions, or as a source of rubber, tin, and oil, or as furnishing human chattels to work the raw materials. The Atlantic Charter, first enunciated by Roosevelt and Churchill and later adopted by all the United Nations, may prove to be the Magna Carta of economic justice, which must be made a living reality.

We now know that political freedom and economic justice are by themselves illusory and fleeting except in an atmosphere of international security. It may have taken our tribal ancestors uncounted ages before police and law courts were invented to keep order among individuals; difficult it may well be, but why must we regard as hopeless police and law courts among nations to dispense justice and enforce law and order as with individuals?

My people have been most loyal supporters of the defunct League of Nations, to whose tribunals we brought our case when our national life was endangered. Past failures have not dimmed our hopes that an effective world instrument to dispense and enforce justice will arise from the terrors and sufferings and sacrifices of this war, and for such an international government China, with all other liberty-loving nations, will gladly cede such of its sovereign powers as may be required.

Where, in the foregoing statement, is there a hint of any ominous intentions of China's using its power potential to upset the peace of the world? And how many other nations have as courageously pledged a willingness to surrender a portion of their sovereign rights in the interests of continuing peace and genuine international security?

China is strong now, of course. Japan has found China dismayingly strong since July of 1937—but her strength is for defense, not for offense. Industrial effectiveness is the prime essential today for aggressive military strength. Nations cannot wage modern warfare without magnificently organized factory systems, great skill and much experience in technology, and huge, accessible stores of resources.

China today has pitifully few factories. She has only a short railway system, lacks highways, has no navy and no merchant marine. China has never yet made an airplane or an automobile or a truck. It has taken the United States, with all of its equipment and advantages, more than two years to become geared to efficient war production; it would take China two decades. Cynics may, if they choose, distrust China's announced good intentions, but they cannot well disregard the physical handicaps which would prevent China from becoming an aggressor even if she were so minded. It is a certain sign of outdated thinking to argue that when the peace is made we must not permit Japan to be weakened lest China's growing strength upset the "balance of power."

Under the Treaty of Shimonoseki, after the 1894-95 war against China, Japan was ceded the large and rich semi-tropical island of Formosa and the string of islands once known as the Pescadores, and now renamed by Japan the Ryukyu Islands. Formosa must be returned to China. It flanks the South China coast, Hongkong and Canton, and menaces the near-by Philippines. The natives are Chinese and have known no liberalism or generosity of treatment during nearly fifty years of Japanese rule.

Because of Formosa's proximity to the Chinese coast, Japan has always claimed a special interest in near-by Fukien Province and has sought to dominate the north-eastern portion of bordering Kwangtung. The Japanese traders and military have freely used the criminal element of the Formosans for years to filter into the Chinese mainland, particularly at Swatow, Amoy, and Foochow. Whenever these worthies got into trouble with the Chinese for smuggling or other offenses, the Japanese have made an issue of each case, claiming for the culprits the protection of extraterritoriality because they were Japanese subjects.

On Formosa the Japanese created huge Army and Navy bases, and it was from that island that most of the bombers came which blasted Hongkong and Manila, and it was from there and from Chinese-owned Hainan Island that most of the invading troops were launched against the Philippines.

The Pescadores completely flank the Chinese coast between the southern tip of Japan proper and the northern tip of Formosa. Ownership of these islands and control of the channels between enabled Japan to close the China Sea to the navies of the United Nations and to lengthen her communication lines far to the south with complete impunity. These "floating fortresses," like Formosa, must be returned to China, and in the interest of continued peace should be disarmed.

China does not want Korea, never owned Korea, and now would not have it as a gift; so the case of the future of the one-time Hermit Kingdom properly falls into a separate chapter, even though the Korean rulers long paid annual tribute to the Chinese emperors at Peking.

The case of Manchuria, however, vitally concerns China. Already in this country there are evidences of differences of opinion concerning Manchuria's future. Some quarters put forth the argument that Manchuria should be awarded to Japan, others advocate autonomy under Japanese guidance, while still others recommend an independent state under international control for a period of years and later a plebiscite to decide eventual national allegiance.

Arguments against freeing Manchuria entirely from Japanese control are many and include the fact that Japan has spent many billion yen on the economic development of these northeastern provinces, and also the fact that nearly 750,000 Japanese civilians have settled there during the last decade and are therefore entitled to spend the rest of their lives under the rule of their Empire. These are queer arguments to justify the forcible theft of a territory 504,-000 square miles in extent, which has a total population of more than 35,000,000, of whom 32,000,000 are Chinese and the rest Manchus, Mongolians, and Japanese. Must 32,000,-000 Chinese spend the rest of their lives under Japanese rule just because 750,000 unwanted Japanese have settled in their midst with the backing of Tokyo's soldiers and financing by heavy Japanese Government subsidies?

For the last fifteen years Japan and hired Japanese propagandists have been busy spreading the fiction that Manchuria was never a part of China and that there is no historical justification for China's insistence upon a return of

sovereignty there. The commission of enquiry headed by
Lord Lytton, which was sent to the Far East by the League
of Nations in 1932, spent much time investigating Manchuria's actual status and in its final report had this to say
about this debated topic:

Manchuria has, since the dawn of history, been inhabited by
various Tungus tribes, who mixed freely with Mongol Tartars.
Under the influence of Chinese immigrants of superior civilization they learned to organize themselves, and established several
kingdoms which sometimes dominated the greater part of
Manchuria and some of the northern districts in China and
Korea. The Liao, Chin and Manchu dynasties even conquered
large parts or the whole of China over which they ruled for
centuries.

China, on the other hand, under strong Emperors, was able
to stem the tide from the north, and in her turn to establish
sovereignty over large parts of Manchuria. Colonization by
Chinese settlers was practiced at a very early date. . . . For
two thousand years a permanent foothold has been maintained,
and Chinese culture has always been active in the southernmost
part of Manchuria. The influence of this culture had become
very strong during the rule of the Ming dynasty (1368 to
1644), whose authority extended over practically the whole of
Manchuria.

The Manchus were permeated with Chinese culture, and
had amalgamated to a great extent with the Chinese before they
overthrew the Ming administration in Manchuria in 1616, and
in 1628 passed the Great Wall to conquer China. In the

Manchu army were large numbers of Chinese who were organized in separate military units known as Chinese Banners.

The Lytton report follows the relationship between China and Manchuria down through the centuries, points out that the Manchu language was virtually replaced by the Chinese, and that when, in 1911, the revolution began and the Chinese Republic was established, the Manchurian authorities all accepted the *fait accompli*.

Manchuria is so thoroughly Chinese, and the Japanese are so thoroughly hated there, that if every measure of Japanese interest is not relinquished, and if the Japanese settlers are not repatriated, the Manchurian question will remain more of a peril to the peace of East Asia than Alsace and Lorraine have been to Europe since the Franco-Prussian War of 1870.

To plead the cause of the 750,000 Japanese immigrants is the height of absurdity. They were sent to Manchuria as part of the Army's policy. In most cases individuals and whole villages were heavily subsidized. Free passage was given to each settler and his family, free land was waiting, and individual Government loans ranged from 1,000 to 5,000 yen per head of family. In each village the Japanese Government maintained free schools, a veterinary, a doctor, and regional hospitals, and gave free seed to the transplanted farmers. Considering this lavish subsidy system, the accomplishment of settling less than 750,000 people in Manchuria in more than a decade proves the absurdity of Japan's claim that she must have this vast and rich area to accommodate her surplus population.

Against this poor Japanese record stands the fact that, in the decade before the Japanese conquest began in 1931, the movement of entirely voluntary Chinese immigrants into Manchuria had reached a total of more than 1,000,000 a year. They flooded northward from the overpopulated provinces of Hopei and Shantung, and they received no Chinese Government aid of any kind.

To give Japan Manchuria just because she overran it with her armies and invested huge sums of money there would mean to China what it would mean to the United States to be robbed of one sixth of our area inhabited by more than 8,500,000 Americans. Moreover, the alienation of Manchuria would take from China about 40 per cent of her coal and iron reserves and most of her grazing lands and the areas to which she looks for horses and cattle, besides the great and fertile plains which produce essential grains like soybeans, millet, and wheat. In addition, the Manchurian forests contain nearly 50 per cent of all of China's standing timber.

The province of Jehol, historically a part of China, has been included under the Manchurian administration by the Japanese. This province, too, must be given back to China. It is rich in coal and iron and other minerals. Aside from mining development Japan has used Jehol for little except the growth of the opium poppy, and most of the opium which debauches the Chinese people in Japanese-occupied areas, and which helps to enrich Japanese generals, comes from this province.

Japan will object bitterly to being evicted from Manchuria. She has invested at least ten billion yen in the country—and most of it was spent there when the yen was worth nearly 50 cents in American money. Railways, harbors, mines, smelters, great manufacturing concerns, extensive heavy industries, airports and air lines, schools, hospitals —these are some of the things into which Japanese money has been poured. Some of them have returned handsome profits, and some have involved heavy losses. So extensive has been the industrial development that Manchuria has been made into Japan's secondary arsenal—an arsenal of such importance that without it she could not have fought China since 1937 and could not have attacked the democracies in the Far Pacific.

China will claim that all these Japanese investments in Manchuria must be surrendered in lieu of an indemnity, and that even though the sums they represent are vast they will not serve to compensate adequately for the loss of life and the ruin, destruction, and desolation which Japan has spread far and wide in China since the "incident" was begun at Marco Polo Bridge, near Peiping, on July 7, 1937. China has repeatedly said that she will fight on until she regains control of Manchuria and liberates the 35,000,000 people held in alien bondage there. Presumably it will be Chinese armies which will defeat Japanese armies on the plains near Mukden. If that occurs, the fate of Manchuria will be settled automatically.

But whether Chinese armies actually drive out the Japanese or not, the United States has been bound for a decade not to accede to continuing Japanese control of Manchuria. It was our Government which, in 1932, injected a new moral sanction into international affairs. We declared that we would never recognize territorial changes gained by aggression. For ten years we have adhered closely to this declaration and have never in any way recognized any legality in Japan's new position in Manchuria, nor have we treated the so-called Manchukuo Empire even as a *de facto* state. So scrupulous has our State Department been in this matter that even our consular officials in Manchuria have been technically accredited to the Chinese Government, although China has had no shadow of authority there since late in 1931.

Captious critics who say that the United States has "never had a real Far Eastern policy" forget that since the Washington Conference of 1921–22 our Government has never swerved from insistence on observing "the territorial and administrative integrity of China." Had we been willing to relax this policy, we would probably not be at war with Japan today.

CHAPTER V

China and Her Allies

COMPLETE JUSTICE FOR CHINA will by no means have
been realized merely by ousting Japan from the Asiatic
mainland and by making restitution to China of Manchuria,
Jehol, Formosa, and the Pescadores. Other restitutions will
be in order, and for the first time in modern history China
must be granted a status of complete freedom and equality
with other nations—must be conceded complete sovereignty
within her own domains.

This means that all the settlements and concessions in
China must be handed over, without reservations, to Chinese sovereignty and administration. It means that the old
privileges of maintaining foreign garrisons on Chinese soil,
foreign warships in Chinese rivers, and foreign trading
ships on China's coastal and river trading routes must all
be surrendered. Already, on October 9th of 1942, the

United States and Britain had made belated announcement of intention to relinquish extraterritorial rights, which had then been in effect a few months more than 100 years. After the war all foreigners who choose to live or do business in China will have to live under Chinese law and under the jurisdiction of China's courts and judges, instead of living under their own foreign laws and being amenable only to their own consular courts.

The American-British joint announcement of intention to surrender extraterritoriality was not, unhappily, accompanied by any announcement of intention to give up other special treaty and concession rights, and there has been no hint of any plan for the restitution of all alienated Chinese territory.

China knows what she is fighting for. But China does not yet know what the United Nations are fighting for, except such generalities as self-preservation, the complete defeat of the three Axis Powers, and the creation of a vague thing called "the better world of the future."

China wants and is entitled to complete equality of status with the other great nations of the world, and also to the complete restoration of her territorial integrity as it existed before European imperialism began to attempt dismemberment of the Chinese Empire a century ago. To the logical Chinese mind there is no sense in the United Nations' being determined to force Japan to relinquish all her concessions, leases, and conquests in China, while at the same time

China's allies, the United Nations, make no declaration that individual nations of that group will also hand back to China all the territory they have filched from her during past periods of decadent helplessness.

The Japanese Army is today in possession of the famous International Settlement and French Concession at Shanghai. It holds the Legation Quarter at Peiping, the foreign concessions at Tientsin and Hankow, the island of Kulangsu at Amoy, and the island of Shameen at Canton. It would be preposterous for American and British forces to assist China in driving the Japanese from these places and then say to the Chinese, "These still belong to us; you may not administer affairs here." If we were to attempt an absurd injustice of that kind we would probably be driven out by force, for China's mood will brook no injustices in the day of victory. And the Chinese still remember the injustices of the Treaty of Versailles and the powerlessness of the League of Nations when Japan invaded Manchuria.

What this complete liberation of China from foreign bondage to alien powers will mean to the Chinese people can scarcely be conceived in this country. This liberation will have required participation in two world wars and years of agitation and armed resistance against the Japanese, but that it will have been well worth the price can be understood only when the measure of China's former helplessness is clearly understood.

In the summer of 1914, before the first World War

started, China was subject to the following foreign penetrations and dominations:

Beginning in the far north, Russia owned the Chinese Eastern Railway, a system more than 1,000 miles in length running across northern Manchuria. This railway ownership included the right to keep armed soldiers along the right of way and also carried ownership and a virtual monopoly of river shipping, telephones, and telegraphs.

Japan owned the South Manchuria Railway, then 695 miles in length, running from Dairen in the south up through Mukden to Changchun, with a branch to the Korean border. Japan also held a 99-year lease on the tip of the Kwangtung Peninsula, with the ports of Dairen and Port Arthur, and was operating great coal mines and other enterprises. Her railway holding, under treaty, permitted her to keep a maximum of 15,000 soldiers along the railway zone to guard the line and preserve order.

In 1914 China's maritime customs was dominated by foreigners, and the collection and distribution of customs money was under foreign control. Her railways were mortgaged to the hilt, and her salt taxes were collected and disbursed by foreigners. Her postal system was under the direction of a foreign staff, and many of the Treaty Powers, including the United States, maintained their own post offices on Chinese soil. China did not enjoy tariff autonomy, and her import tariffs were limited to 5 and 7½ per cent.

In what was then Peking the United States, Britain,

Japan, Germany, France, Italy, and Belgium maintained their own Army or Navy garrisons, with the right to operate the railway from the then capital to the port of Chingwantao. At Tientsin, Britain, France, Germany, Italy, Russia, and Belgium had their own concessions and the privilege of maintaining armed forces therein.

Britain held Weihaiwei under lease and planned to make it into a naval station. Germany held a long lease on Tsingtao and the Kiaochow Bay region, had heavily fortified it and used it as a naval base, and owned the 280-mile railway leading inland to Tsinan, the Shantung provincial capital.

At Shanghai were the International Settlement and the French Concession, and large foreign military forces were maintained there. Up the Yangtze River above Shanghai there were foreign concessions at Chinkiang and at Kiukiang, and at Hankow the British, Germans, Russians, French, and Japanese had large and important concession areas.

Southward of Shanghai, along the coast, there was an International Settlement on Kulangsu Island in the harbor of Amoy, the British and French concessions divided the island of Shameen in the Pearl River at Canton, Britain held Hongkong, the Portuguese held Macao, and France held Kwangchowan, the site for a great naval base.

In China's ports and rivers were to be found naval craft and the merchant ships of the United States, Britain, Germany, France, Japan, and Italy, and wherever the concession areas were located the Treaty Powers could send their armed forces at will.

Americans—both civilians and the armed forces—most Europeans, Mexicans, and some South Americans as well as the Japanese were not under the jurisdiction of Chinese laws or courts. They lived in China under the laws of their own countries and were tried or sued in their own courts or in consular courts before consular officials of their own nationalities.

It will be a far cry from this previous condition of penetration and servitude to absolute freedom and equality among the peoples and nations of the world, but China will demand this and will no doubt receive it in full measure when the United Nations have won the war.

Is there any valid argument against an immediate announcement by all the United Nations that China is to be given freedom and equality on the day of victory? Such a declaration would not only hearten the people of Free China, but greatly encourage those who are in areas now under Japanese military occupation. And the effect upon the millions of Chinese in the Philippines, in Siam, in Malaya, in Burma, and in the East Indies would be tremendous.

British Hongkong and Portuguese Macao are different problems. Hongkong was ceded to Britain and has been

a crown colony and·an integral part of the British Empire
for just a century. It was acquired in 1842 by the Treaty
of Nanking, which ended the so-called Opium Wars.

The Portuguese have been in Macao for 380 years, since
they persuaded China to recognize it as a leased territory
in 1563. Since the close of the era of sailing-ship days, and
particularly since the British made Hongkong into one of
the great seaports of the world, the importance of Macao
has steadily declined. Before Japan precipitated the general
war in the Pacific, Macao was little more than a center for
vice, smuggling, gambling, and the opium trade. It has long
been a plague spot on the South China coast and should be
surrendered. Macao's value to Portugal ceased being political or economic long ago, and the governors and other
appointive officials sent out from Portugal for unnamed
political debts or exploits have done nothing to clean up the
little island city. The area is only eleven square miles, and
the population was about 170,000 at the last census in 1933.

It will be difficult for the British Crown to surrender
Hongkong, which for a hundred years has been the far
Pacific outpost and symbol of the greatness of the Empire.
But that is all Hongkong would be in the future—a symbol,
and a trading point to drain a major share of the profits of
South China's economic life.

Before the days of the airplane's efficiency as bomber,
fighter, and troop carrier, Hongkong was considered nearly
as powerful a fortress and naval base as Gibraltar. The

guns of the island and mainland batteries made Hongkong hazardous of approach from the sea, and the waters west of the main island afforded an admirable shelter for surface naval craft and submarines. But the airplane changed Hongkong from an almost invulnerable military and naval base to a position of extreme weakness. Hongkong, the little island nine miles wide and eleven miles long, lacks streams, and the springs are small. Small dams impounded rain water in small reservoirs, and aerial bombers blasted these dams. The water ran into the sea, and there was nothing for more than 1,000,000 people to drink or to use in fighting fires.

Hongkong's great commercial value arises from the fact that it is the only fine deep-water harbor on the South China coast. Amoy and Swatow, to the northward, are small and shallow. Canton is on the silted, tidal portion of the Pearl River, and nothing larger than a 3,000-ton freighter can navigate that far inland. The proposed development of a Chinese-owned port at Whampoa, on the river below Canton, would cost $40,000,000, and such a project would be unnecessary if Hongkong belonged to China.

Britain held an area of 391 square miles at Hongkong, for in addition to the island itself she held a 99-year lease on the tip of Kowloon Peninsula on the mainland. Less than a mile and a half of water separates Hongkong from Kowloon, and many of the great docks and warehouses were built on the Kowloon side. From Kowloon to Canton there is rail connection, and before the "incident" began in 1937 it was possible to go by rail from Kowloon to Peiping—or on to Berlin or Paris, for that matter, for there is rail connection from Peiping through Manchuria and on to the trans-Siberian system. Thanks to the tenacity and skill of the Chinese defense of Changsha, which the Japanese have attacked with ferocity four times, Japan has never yet been able to re-establish through rail traffic between South and North China.

Not only will it be a blow to Britain's prestige in Asia to surrender title of Hongkong to China, but it will be a sentimental wrench as well. The plea will be made that since thousands of British, Canadian, and Indian troops drenched the island and the forts on The Peak with their blood when they died fighting off the Japanese, Hongkong is "forever a part of England." Well, it is equally "forever a part of China," too. Chinese volunteers died in large numbers defending Hongkong, and thousands of Chinese civilians were slaughtered by the bombings and shellings. On the mainland, in vain but valiant attempts to check the Japanese advance down the Kowloon Peninsula, thousands of regular Chinese troops were killed and wounded before the great British outpost capitulated.

Regardless of the eventual British attitude, which mere expediency should dictate as one of co-operation and generosity, China will be mindful of her new strength and greatness and will demand that which she considers just.

Already China is proudly conscious of the fact that she has successfully withstood determined Japanese attacks for more than five years, while Britain, America, and Holland were pushed clear out of the Far East by the Japanese in only a third of a year. China is proud and conscious of the important fact that when the British were routed in Burma it was Chinese re-enforcements that checked the Japanese sufficiently to permit the retreating British to complete their scorched-earth policy and retire without utter destruction or mass surrender.

Unhappily there are many persons in this country and in Britain, too, who look askance upon the surrender of extraterritoriality and upon any project for complete restitution of all rights and territories wrested from China since the period of imperialistic expansion was begun in the Far East more than a century ago. Judging the future by the past, which is not always sound, they predict that after the pressure of Japanese invasion is released China will relapse again into civil wars and chaos, or that failing this she will develop into as arrogant and expansionist a power as Japan has been.

Of course there is danger of revolution and civil war in China. Any prolonged period of conflict is likely to be followed by internal disorders in any country. The Czarist Government of Russia was far stronger in 1914 than General Chiang Kai-shek's Government is today, and yet Russia collapsed into rebellion, civil war, and chaos; and there have been many other instances of a similar aftermath to war.

Admittedly there are today in China only partially reconciled leaders and cliques who still nourish grievances which originated during the civil wars which preceded the Japanese attack. There is also the grave and continuing problem of a complete reconciliation of the Chinese Communist party and army and the Central Government.

Assuming a victory for the United Nations, China will probably emerge from the war with an Army of four or five million hardened veterans. She will face problems of impoverishment, famine, unemployment. Many of the great cities are already half in ruins, and more will be shelled and bombed and burned before the day of victory. China's industries, like our own, will be geared to war production, her merchant marine will be almost non-existent, and her meager railway mileage will be in ruins.

China, victorious, will have to have help and credits, food and machinery, and the best service our industrial and economic experts can offer. If any of these are withheld, then indeed there may be chaos, and if territorial, political, and economic justice are denied there will be bitter resentment and probably violence.

China will need enormous loans, mostly in the form of the goods and machinery required for rehabilitation and industrialization. Our heavy industry should long have an outlet to the China market; for one thing, her railways will have to be largely rebuilt, almost completely re-equipped, and should be greatly extended.

Nowhere else in the world is there a country of similar size, population, natural resources, industry, and thrift which will need our help in such great measure. It will be to our own self-interest to take all possible measures to maintain internal stability in China and to ward off any collapse into chaos. "The great China market," which has been the dream of imperialism for more than a century, can become a reality after this war if it is developed in co-operation with the Chinese, and this market should play a great part in helping to cushion our own difficult turn-over from war production to peace production and should help to prevent colossal postwar unemployment in this country.

The Chinese have had a bitter time of it. They will probably not again countenance the use of such dangerous weapons as anti-race movements, boycotts, and other devices by irresponsible organizations acting for political ends. The Chinese are amongst the most astute traders and businessmen in the world, and they realize that investments will be made in proportion to the degree of law and order they maintain in their own land. And the terrible retribution which will have overtaken Japan in the day of defeat will be a deterrent, for at least a generation, of any impulse toward aggression or expansion at the cost of weaker neighbors.

This is not the end of the catalogue of serious problems concerning China which will have to be met with the coming of peace, but unequivocal declarations of intentions concerning the settlement of the foregoing issues would have a tremendous effect on China's morale and would also have profound repercussions in India, in the East Indies, and elsewhere in Asia.

Other problems to be faced and equitably settled by the eventual peace will be our own Exclusion Act, Australia's "white man's continent" policy, and in particular China's interest in the tremendous Chinese populations living overseas.

The last official census of Chinese living overseas gave the total as 7,838,895, a figure which took no account of about 5,000,000 Formosans, or of nearly 1,000,000 Chinese living under British rule in Hongkong. Since the latter will presumably return to live under Chinese sovereignty at the close of the war, the other large and important Chinese groups living under other flags are about 2,500,000 in Siam, 1,700,000 in Malaya, and nearly 1,500,000 in the Netherlands East Indies. In the continental United States there are about 75,000 Chinese, in the Philippines 110,500, and in Hawaii another 27,000.

The overseas Chinese have been important to China in an economic sense for many years. Chinese in Hawaii and on the American mainland formerly sent many millions of dollars to their families at home every year, and the same was true of the large Chinese colonies in Malaya and in the East Indies. The Chinese in Siam, for instance, sent $34,-200,000 in Chinese money to the district around Swatow in 1929, but the depression years saw this total dwindle to $14,900,000 by 1933. These bulky remittances from abroad did much to help China maintain a balance of trade.

During the years just prior to the Japanese attack in 1937 the Chinese Government showed a growing interest in the welfare and loyalty of these great overseas colonies. In some cases monthly appropriations were made by the Government to help maintain purely Chinese schools in foreign countries, but in the main the endeavors of Nanking were confined to safeguarding equality of treatment for Chinese living abroad and to assist in assuring them the rights to peaceful trade and safe living conditions.

The future of the American people is now bound up with the future of China. In addition to the pledges of the Atlantic Charter and the joint pledge of the thirty-two United Nations, our Secretary of War and Secretary of Navy, on the fifth anniversary of Japan's attack upon China, issued an Order of The Day which, after recalling the "gallant resistance . . . tenacity and courage" of the Chinese, closes with this paragraph:

"Today the members of the Army and Navy of the United States salute their comrades-in-arms in China, and join with them in the firm determination to expel the aggressor from every foot of Chinese soil."

We will carry out that pledge, of course; and it is un‑ thinkable that after it has been fulfilled we will leave China to face alone and unaided the desperate problems which the peace will bring.

CHAPTER VI

Freedom—to Be Earned

O<small>NE</small> of the most loudly vocal claimants for independence after a United Nations victory will be Korea, which has endured nearly four decades of Japanese domination and more than thirty years of inclusion as part of the Japanese Empire. This means that Korea has had nearly two fifths of a century of slavery and greedy exploitation to endure, and slavery and exploitation under Japanese rule are a terrible experience for any people to undergo.

The measure of Korea's suffering and the length of her enslavement would seem to merit the rich reward of immediate independence, but actually the Korean people are not now fit or ready to govern themselves. Various cliques and factions, some genuinely patriotic, others hypocritical and self-seeking, will raise a tremendous outcry and will charge the United Nations with instigating a new tyrannical imperialism when Korea is denied immediate independence; but the denial must be made, not only in the interests of peace and security in the Orient, but in the interests of the Korean people themselves.

Immediate freedom from Japanese domination the Koreans must have, as a minimum of human justice, but they are not ready to rule themselves with stability and success, so independence must be denied them until they have been educated to the point where they can earn the right to manage their own affairs.

To most Americans Korea is merely "another one of those Asiatic countries," and knowledge of what Korea really is, what its history has been, and how it became annexed to the Japanese Empire are unread pages in the history of the world.

Korea is a peninsula jutting out from the northeastern coast of the Asiatic mainland. Except for a few miles in the north, near Vladivostok, its only land frontier is that adjoining Manchuria. It has an area of 85,228 square miles, which means that it is larger than Kansas but smaller than Oregon. Kansas has a population of around 2,000,000, and Oregon has a population of a little more than 1,000,000. But Korea has a population of about 24,000,000 Koreans, and not many more than 250,000 Japanese civilians.

In addition to the 24,000,000 Koreans living in what was once their own land, there are another 2,000,000 in Manchuria, where they went to find a measure of freedom before Japan grabbed that disputed area and again brought them under the yoke of slavery. In the Soviet Maritime Provinces there are about 300,000 more Koreans, and at least an equal number in China. There are also fairly large Korean groups in the United States, in Hawaii, and in Formosa, and all told the Korean people probably number nearly 27,000,000.

Almost without exception those living beyond the range of Japanese tyranny are ardent advocates of Korean independence and give the independence movement financial support. Tens of thousands of the Koreans in Manchuria and in China are openly in arms against Japan, either in Chinese or Korean armies or in important guerrilla bands, and the Koreans in Soviet Siberia are, in the main, active as plotters or spies or underground workers against continued Japanese domination of their homeland.

Korea, in the last decade of the last century, was one of the most backward and most corrupt countries in all of the Orient. The imperial dynasty was decadent, the nobility was ignorant, bigoted, and greedy, officialdom was dishonest and utterly inefficient.

For centuries the Korean emperors had paid tribute to the Chinese emperors at Peking, and it was a dispute over China's right to send troops there to restore order which led to the Sino-Japanese War of the 1890s. Then Czarist Russia, having obtained from China the right to build a railway across Manchuria and down to Port Arthur, became a competitor for the overlordship of Korea, and it was this clash of interests which brought about the Russo-Japanese War of 1904–05.

Victorious Japan was in military occupation of the Korean peninsula when the war ended, and she has remained in occupation ever since. First Japan proclaimed a protectorate over Korea and then, in 1910, formally annexed the one-time Hermit Kingdom, thus seemingly bringing to a definite conclusion centuries of intermittent strife.

Our own acquiescence in this annexation and Britain's actual connivance at the step are disgraceful chapters in international history. Japan had repeatedly pledged herself to respect Korea's sovereignty and independence, and the United States had given Korea assurances of support which Korea considered binding.

Britain permitted Japan to annex Korea as part of the price she paid for the binding Anglo-Japanese alliance, which at that time helped to check German expansion in the Far East and enabled the removal from the Orient to European waters of important portions of the British Fleet, which were urgently needed there as the power of Germany under the last Kaiser became menacingly great.

The United States signed a treaty of perpetual peace and friendship with Korea, which today furnishes melancholy reading. One paragraph specified:

"If other powers deal unjustly or oppressively with either Government, the other will exert their good offices."

Japan invaded Korea as long ago as during the reign of the Empress Jingo, about A.D. 200. As late as the time of the supremacy of the great Shogun Hideyoshi, who died in 1598, Japan attempted the conquest of the eastern part of the Asiatic mainland. The plan called for the invasion and subjugation first of Korea, then of Manchuria, and finally of China, but combined Chinese and Korean armies administered a crushing defeat to the Japanese before the first stage of this ambitious program had been completed.

For the last half-century Japan has likened the Korean peninsula to "a dagger pointed at the heart of the Japanese Empire." Actually, the dagger has been pointed the other way, and Korea has been the convenient springboard for Japan's invasions of the Asiatic mainland. Fifty years ago Japan began strengthening her hold upon Korea by tactics since made familiar in China and by Hitler in his moves of a few years ago against Czechoslovakia and Poland. Japanese thugs would create riots and disturbances at Seoul or Chemulpo, and then Japanese cruisers and troop transports would go rushing across the Tsushima Strait to "restore order" in Korea.

Finally Japanese daggers were actually used in the Korean imperial palace: the Empress was murdered by the Japanese military, and palace intrigue and intimidation eventually led to the imprisonment and abdication of the dynasty. Today the legitimate descendant of Korea's ancient line of rulers is not even a pretender to the throne. He was taken to Japan, educated there, given a Japanese pension, a Japanese name, and a Japanese wife. His position today is even more tragic than that of Pu Yi, one-time "Boy Emperor of China," whom the Japanese dragged from retirement in Tientsin and now keep immured in a shoddy palace at Hsinching under the Japanese-imposed title of Kang Teh, Emperor of Manchukuo.

In fairness to the Japanese it must be conceded that in a material sense they have done a magnificent job in Korea. When they took it over the country was filthy, unhealthy, and woefully poverty-stricken. The mountains had been denuded of their forests, the valleys were subject to recurrent floods, decent roads were non-existent, illiteracy was prevalent, and typhoid, smallpox, cholera, dysentery, and the plague were epidemic annually.

Today the mountains are reforested; the railway, telephone, and telegraph systems are excellent; the public-health service is highly efficient; good highways abound; flood-control and irrigation works have vastly increased the food production, and fine harbors have been developed and are well managed. The country has become so prosperous and so healthy that the 1905 population of 11,000,-000 has risen to 24,000,000, and the average scale of living is today almost immeasurably higher than it was at the turn of the century.

But this health, this relative prosperity, this material improvement of Korea, has not been instituted for the benefit of the Korean people. Disease has been stamped out because a sick people cannot produce bountifully for their conquerors. Living standards have been raised for the same reason that a farmer feeds his stock well—they can do more work. All the profits from Korea are and have been for forty years siphoned off to Japan.

If Japan had been half as solicitous for the welfare of the people of Korea as she has been for the productivity of the peninsula, there would probably be little bitterness and unrest. Instead, Japan has ruthlessly oppressed the millions of hapless and helpless natives of this ancient kingdom, which has an authentic history stretching back 4,200 years in contrast to Japan's fictitious and absurd claim to descent from the "Sun Goddess" a little more than 2,600 years ago.

In Korea any Japanese may beat or spit upon any Korean. Any Japanese may force any Korean into selling his land or his business for a mere pittance. The idea of social equality for the Korean is met with derision, and the idea of equality before the law is considered preposterous. Korean homes may be entered and searched at any time without warrant or valid excuse.

In the schools the teaching of the Korean language is barred, and no Korean is able to obtain in his own land the equivalent to a third- or fourth-year high-school education in this country. The Japanese police possess judicial powers, and flog, imprison, and fine Korean civilians at will. No appeal is possible, and there no longer exist any Korean newspapers in which the grievances of the natives of the peninsula may be set forth. The Japanese-owned and staffed railways deliver damaged crates and broken merchandise to a Korean shopowner, but crates and goods arrive intact for his Japanese competitor next door. For years the Japanese attempted to foster the use of cheap opium by the Korean people, but the oppressed millions, sensing the official plan for debauchery and ruin, continued in their temperate ways, and few have become addicts.

Christian missionaries, most of them from the United States and Great Britain, did what they could to alleviate the lot of the Koreans and gave them such education as the Japanese overlords permitted. But now all Christian organizations have been banned; the Japanese Government has seized and closed all mission schools, hospitals, and churches, and the foreigners have been imprisoned or banished. Korean Christian groups have been threatened with severe reprisals if the missionaries, on returning to their home countries, reveal the truth about conditions as they exist in Korea.

Japan rules Korea through a governor general who is responsible only to the Emperor and to the heads of the Japanese Army. The administration is, in fact, an army-police dictatorship, assisted by swarms of spies and bolstered by an army of occupation. The police and even the Japanese school teachers wear swords, as symbols of their supremacy.

In the long history of Japanese rule there has been no evidence of any attempt to placate this helpless and disarmed people by any showing of justice or humanity, and as a result it is Japan's own fault that nearly unanimously the 24,000,000 Koreans in their own homeland would fight against her tomorrow if they had any means of obtaining arms. In fact there are sporadic uprisings and campaigns of sabotage, in spite of the hopelessness of such movements under present conditions, and in spite of the fact that those who participate know in advance the kind and measure of barbarous punishment which will follow detection.

The peaceful and unarmed demonstrations in favor of freedom in 1919, when the Koreans placed faith in President Wilson's promise of "self-determination," resulted in 7,501 executions and mass killings and in the imprisonment of more than 2,000,000 of the demonstrators. The cruelties of that period, akin to the atrocities that occurred at Nanking in December of 1937, shocked the civilized world. There was another hopeless uprising in 1929, also punished with Draconian severity.

Since the "China incident" developed into a long-drawn stalemate, Japan has been dragooning young Koreans into the Japanese Army, and Chinese sources estimate that about 150,000 Korean troops have been sent to various zones of conflict. But the Japanese dare not trust these troops and, as a result, place one Japanese to every nine Koreans in the ranks, and all the commissioned and non-commissioned officers are Japanese. Moreover, Korean contingents are always flanked on both sides by Japanese contingents, and there are several known authentic instances in which the Japanese have had to turn their machine guns against the uniformed Koreans to quell mutinies and mass attempts at desertion.

The indignities which the Japanese have inflicted upon the Koreans are almost beyond belief. Even Korean place and street names have been changed to Japanese names. The old imperial palace, or Forbidden City, at Seoul (renamed Keijo by the conquerors) is now overrun with weeds and is being permitted to go to ruin. The Korean equivalent to Peiping's Temple of Heaven has been made into a tea-drinking pavilion for the use of guests at Seoul's leading hotel. When the courageous Empress was murdered by Japanese, her body was wrapped in oil-soaked garments and burned in a palace courtyard close to the Emperor's living quarters. And after this crime an edict was promulgated, falsely purported to come from the Emperor, degrading the dead consort to the status of a prostitute.

But the deposed Emperor had courage. When the question of Korean independence came to the fore during the making of the Treaty of Versailles, the Japanese produced what purported to be a petition signed by thousands of

Koreans expressing the wish to remain under Japanese "protection." Some of the signatures were genuine—there are Quislings in all lands—but most of them were forged, and those not forged had been signed at the point of the bayonet. The ex-Emperor was directed to sign, too, but refused to do so. Three days later he died—poisoned.

Strategically Korea is of the utmost importance in the Far East. On the west is the Yellow Sea, on the south the China Sea, and on the east the Sea of Japan. The distance from Moji in Japan to Fusan, the great Korean port, is only a little more than 160 miles across the Tsushima Strait. The peninsula has 1,700 miles of coast line, many fine natural harbors, and numerous mountainous outlying islands. The iron, coal, copper, silver, and gold mines of Korea have been of extreme importance to Japan. There are also mines giving small yields of tungsten, zinc, lead, and graphite—all important in time of war. The bountiful crops of rice, millet, cotton, wheat, and soybeans enrich Japan's larder and pocketbook, and the Korean fisheries are extremely productive and contribute to Japan's national diet.

The country has ample natural wealth and resources to support its own people in comfort, for the Koreans are inherently industrious and thrifty, although these virtues have been impaired by the long years of hopelessness endured under Japanese rule when neither industry nor thrift benefited the native inhabitants. If the Koreans, spurred by freedom, were permitted to work for themselves their toil and their soil and their sea should yield them a sound measure of what the Oriental world knows as prosperity.

But in Korea, as in Manchuria, Japan will have to be ousted entirely, and Japanese investments and holdings of all kinds will have to be declared forfeit. This will be a terrible economic blow for Japan to sustain, but even though the total of wealth thus lost will run into the billions of yen it will not adequately compensate the Koreans for what they have endured from the arrogant Japanese domination and cruelty during the last four decades. If Japan were to be left in ownership of Korean railways, telegraphs, telephones, mines, air fields, and harbor works, these holdings would serve as the basis for a new infiltration and exploitation and would be the causes of deep unrest and eventual abuses and disorders of grave scope.

Already there are in existence three different groups aspiring to and making formal claim to the right to establish an independent government in Korea after the United Nations defeat Japan. These groups maintain headquarters in Chungking, China's wartime capital, in the Siberian Maritime Provinces, under Soviet protection, and in Hawaii. The first-named seems to have the most valid claims to seniority, stability, and influence; it even maintains an "ambassador" at Washington in the person of Dr. Syngman Rhee, who was for a long time President of the Korean Government-in-exile.

The *de facto* exiled Government now enjoying sanctuary

in Chungking held its thirty-third Congress-in-exile at the Chinese capital in September of 1941, elected Chong Pyeng as president, and appointed General Li Ching-tien as commander of the Korean armies in Free China.

These Korean armies, fighting in China with the troops of General Chiang Kai-shek against the Japanese, are all volunteers. The Korean forces are divided into five units and are constantly growing as recruits reach Free China from Korea and from Manchuria. They are supported partly by donations from patriotic Koreans in the United States and in Hawaii and partly by subsidy from the Chungking Government, but they are poorly equipped and poorly clothed. Efforts are being made to obtain cash assistance from the United States or to secure an allotment from the American lend-lease aid to China, to be charged against the Korean Government of the future, but so far Washington has been chary of selecting any favorite amongst the Korean factions.

The Korean regime in Chungking is a branch of the Korean Independent party. On November 15, 1941, the Chinese National Military Council accorded formal recognition of the legal status of the Korean Revolutionary Army in China. In addition to directing the activities of the Korean Army units in Free China, the group in Chungking continually sends secret organizers to work amongst the 2,000,000 Koreans in Manchuria and directs the sabotage and espionage activities of thousands of Koreans who are in the provinces of China under Japanese military occupation.

After the attack on Pearl Harbor the Korean Provisional Government formally declared war against Japan and later made application to be formally recognized as one of the United Nations warring against the Axis Powers; it also seeks formal recognition as the only legal government of Korea.

All these facts would seem to indicate that the Korean Provisional Government at Chungking should at once be accorded recognition, should be invited to sign the pledge of the United Nations, and should be given lend-lease aid in order to enable it to participate more adequately in the fight against Japan. In fact the American State Department has been importuned time and again to do just these things. Fortunately there is accessible for the record a letter written by Secretary of State Cordell Hull on May 20, 1942, in reply to importunities of this kind. Mr. Hull's letter says, in part:

This Government, of course, views with sympathy the aspirations for freedom of the people of Korea, as well as all other peoples now subjugated by the tyranny of Japan and the other Axis powers. . . .

As you are aware, various Korean groups in the United States and in other countries are undertaking to speak for their countrymen in Korea and in areas under Japanese military occupation. A similar situation exists with respect to several other national groups whose countries of origin are under military occupation of the Axis powers. A primary consideration which has guided this Government in dealing with representatives in this country of movements of this character is that it is the desire of this Government to avoid taking action which might, when the victory of the United Nations is achieved, tend to deprive peoples now under the Axis yoke of full freedom to choose and establish their own governments.

The Secretary of State's letter then points out that the problem of the American Government has in some cases been made infinitely complicated and difficult by the lack of unity and by the keen rivalry amongst different groups of one nationality all striving, but not striving together, for the independence of their native land. He concedes that it is a simple thing for an individual to associate himself with any one such group of his own choosing, and then adds:

It is not a simple matter for the Government to commit the United States to a position which involves the preferment of any one alien group over other such groups and an obligation to maintain that preferment regardless of what may be the present or the future wishes of the nation from which that group springs.

Mr. Hull's letter then somewhat tartly takes up what he seems to have considered an implication that if recognition were withheld the aspiring organization would refrain from throwing the full efforts of its supporters into the struggle against Japan. On this point the Secretary of State writes:

> It is difficult to believe that, as you imply, the group for whom you speak does not intend that the nation which they represent shall act on behalf of its freedom until this Government shall first have recognized your group as the *de facto* government of the nation for which they undertake to speak.

Would this not imply—erroneously—that the service of which you speak is "for sale"; that the price is recognition of a certain group by the United States Government, this price to be paid in advance of any action by that nation? I find it indeed difficult to believe that such statements and implications contained in your letter represent the spirit of the people of Korea.

The close of Secretary Hull's letter is very much to the point. It says:

> It is the purpose of this Government that all peoples that are unwillingly subject to the tyranny of aggressor nations shall be given appropriate and practicable aid toward gaining or regaining their freedom. This Government, engaged in an armed struggle which is first of all a struggle in self-defense, welcomes such aid toward a common victory of the peace-loving and law-abiding nations as conquered and suppressed peoples can and will themselves give.

> The United Nations, each and all, are giving in a common

cause. A number of groups representing or speaking for their subjugated fellow countrymen are making important contributions to that cause. It is our hope that all such groups, without exception, will feel impelled to contribute to that cause to the limit of their abilities.

This lucid statement should end the rivalries of various factions which already are striving for place and power and attempting to establish priority positions as the probable governments or administrators of areas which will be freed of alien domination when the United Nations win the war. But unhappily Mr. Hull's clear and concise analysis of the American Government's attitude will not end this kind of strife, and the circumstance that factions are already contending for postwar supremacy indicates the tremendous pressures that will make themselves felt when the time comes for arranging the final terms of peace. These rivalries and strivings are going on not only between Korean groups, but also amongst groups in India and exiled groups representing other peoples whose homelands have been conquered by one or another of the Axis Powers. It is not a heartening spectacle, particularly at a time when victory and defeat are still in the balance.

The generalities of the Atlantic Charter satisfy no one. They are particularly unsatisfactory to the Koreans, who entertained high hopes because of the fine-sounding generalities and vague promises with which President Wilson decorated his speeches and state papers during the first World War.

It is not fair that this long-suffering and disappointed people should be permitted to continue struggling and hoping for something which will not immediately come to pass—independence and self-government. Yet the harsh fact is that decades of Japanese oppression, the lack of general education and training, and factionalism unfit the Korean people for immediate independence. Almost the only Koreans who have had any training in administration are the minor Quislings, who have so little patriotism and self-respect that they accept humiliating positions under their Japanese masters.

Freedom Korea must have as soon as fighting ceases—freedom from the military, political, social, and economic domination of Japan. That should be promised, unequivocally, by the United Nations. Independence should be promised too, but at a later date, after the Koreans have received the education and training necessary for any self-governing people. To give them independence immediately after the close of the war would amount to handing them the dubious gifts of chaos and domestic tyranny.

Sun Yat-sen prescribed a period of "political tutelage" for the Chinese people. The Korean people, too, must receive political tutelage. It may come under an international guardianship, under some successor to the League

of Nations, or, conceivably, under a benevolent protectorate of their own choosing.

Independence and self-government must not only be
earned, they must be carefully guarded. The Korean people
are today not fitted to guard a gift of such inestimable value.

CHAPTER VII

For the Filipinos

It is with grim amusement that the Americans of today can recall the direct and impolite accusations from the great imperialistic powers of Europe that we were "letting the white man down" when we formally promised independence to the Philippine Islands. Our quixotic policy there, it was held, would lead to political unrest and agitation in the rich colonies held in the Far Pacific and in southeast Asia by Britain, France, and the Netherlands, and might even upset India.

Today those same one-time complaining imperialist powers have been driven from all their southeast Asian and South Pacific colonies. Their ousting was not caused by the spread of a desire for independence on the part of colonial peoples, but by the display of brute strength and overwhelming force on the part of an Asiatic power which has grown great not because of the absorption of the political ideas of the West, but because of their utter rejection, and by learning the West's own secrets of militarism and industrialism. The United States has been ousted, too— from the Philippines, and the ousting occurred before we were ready to go, and before the Filipino people were ready to have us leave.

Now the white powers must fight their way back to possession of the colonies which they have lost, but they will achieve this return not to re-establish the old imperialist colonial system, but perforce to grant the very liberty or autonomy to once-subject peoples which they feared those peoples would demand when we made ready to set the Philippines free.

Japan claims to be fighting to free the peoples of East Asia from the domination of the whites. Actually the war she started will terminate in such an emancipation, but only after Japan is defeated and the peoples of East Asia are freed from Japanese oppression. But, curiously, it will be the fact that Japan attacked the democracies which will have greatly hastened the end of the old colonial system. Except in the case of the Philippine Islands, freedom of some kind, whether independence or autonomy, will have been advanced by at least a generation by Japan's policy of aggressive expansion. In the Philippines the war will have served to delay independence for years, unless both we and the Filipinos entirely lose our heads.

The magnitude of the problems involved in this freeing

of tens of millions of peoples of the tropics, most of whom have been under subjection of one kind or another for centuries, staggers the imagination. The mere problem of educating them to the point where they can earn and keep and not misuse their freedom is baffling. The adjustments that must be made to make these people self-supporting, without doing irreparable damage to the economies of America and Europe, may well discourage the world's leading economists and financiers.

It sounds simple and easy to promise the four freedoms to millions of East Asiatics, but only the fatuous-minded optimist can imagine that the problem will be solved merely by driving out and disarming the Japanese, then setting up "governments" after the peoples concerned have selected by plebiscites from jealous and warring factions the men or parties they prefer to govern them. If that were all.

The case of the Philippine Islands is probably the least complicated of all, for in the case of the Philippines there will be no reluctant economic or political groups in the former governing country which will be unready, because of pride, economic need, or political expediency, to relinquish sovereignty. The United States has been ready and willing, since 1935, to give the Filipinos complete independence in 1946, and advance plans were well under way there and here to make the necessary political and economic adjustments.

But the war has basically changed the whole situation.

Hushed are the scandalous voices of our beet-sugar lobby-
ists who favored immediate independence for the Philippines, even though the loss of the free-entry market into
this country for Philippine cane sugar threatened destitu-
tion for millions of the islanders. Hushed, too, is the
angry controversy between naval and military experts as
to whether our position in the Philippines constituted a
strategic weakness or whether Cavite and Corregidor were
mighty bastions which made our interests in the Orient
secure.

How long ago and how childish seem the debates
whether the Filipinos could defend themselves against
aggression, or whether we should seek to neutralize the
islands by a series of treaties, or give the Filipinos a
guaranty of our armed protection when we gave them
their actual independence! And how shameful and inept
seem the assurances given to the Filipino people that "it
can't happen here"!

Freedom the Filipinos must have; absolute independence
if they still want it, after they have estimated the durability
of whatever scheme may be devised for guarding the
peace after this war is ended. Not only have we promised
these things, but by the valiant manner in which the Filipinos assisted us in a hopeless fight against the Japanese
invaders they have earned these things. Freedom will come
to them, not as a gift from the United States, but as a right.

There has been much in our Philippine experiment which

should prove helpful in the future period when, under international guaranties, other backward peoples will have to be trained to earn the right to freedom. Never before in history has there been such a great gamble on the merits of idealism as the forty years we spent attempting to prepare the Filipino people for eventual independence.

We have trained them in the technique of self-government, promoted and taught them a common language to replace more than a score of dialects, and inculcated a respect for the highest ideals of human rights, liberty, and democracy. Since the turn of the century we have aided them to more than double their national income and have taught them the value of public-health services, universal education, good roads, and a sound currency. We received our reward during the grueling retreat southward from Lingayen and during the valiant and hopeless delaying action on Bataan Peninsula. Our faith in the Filipino people and in our own methods of aiding them was magnificently vindicated. And the other colonial powers may well take note of the fact that they had no such help from native Malays, Indonesians, or Burmese as we had from the Filipinos when the Japanese assault came.

The Filipinos learned a lesson, too, during those dire days. Having undergone invasion, rape, and ruin, they will be glad to bear their share of the future burden of keeping their part of the world safe from the aggression of international freebooters.

The future of the Philippine Islands cannot be determined without consideration of neighboring countries and peoples. There are many similarities to be taken into account and many vital differences to be considered, for southern East Asia and the southern islands have all sustained the impact of different and alien cultures.

After three hundred years under Spanish rule, it is only natural that the people of the Philippines are predominantly Catholic, although the southern islands of Sulu and Mindanao are largely Mohammedan and fanatically so. Near by, most of the inhabitants of Java and Malaya are also followers of Islam, but in the East Indies the Protestant Dutch have left their indelible marks. Other portions of the East Indies, however, are largely inhabited by Buddhists and followers of the Hindu religion, and Thailand and Burma and parts of Indo-China have also had their culture greatly influenced by the faiths and the culture of India.

When the United States took over the 7,000 islands of the Philippine group in 1898 after Admiral Dewey had annihilated the Spanish fleet in Manila Bay, this country found itself the owner of a tropical Oriental area 114,000 square miles in extent—about the size of Arizona, or almost exactly twice the size of Michigan. In other words, the land area is as large as that of all of New England plus the states of New York and New Jersey.

Communication was difficult, and the interisland routes were inadequately served by small steamers and sailing vessels. Railways were non-existent, and good roads were few. Racially the people were, and are, a curious blend and mixture. Besides the predominant three strains, Malaysian, Mongoloid, and Negroid, there was the Spanish strain, and also a strong admixture of Chinese, who had been going to the islands and settling and marrying there for centuries.

The population has more than doubled during American occupation, as has the population of Korea during Japanese domination there. But there would be no Korean battalions to aid their conquerors on a Japanese Bataan, and Japan has not educated the Koreans as we have educated the Filipinos —primarily with the aim of preparing them for self-government. This comparison alone blasts Japan's claim to being the "liberator of the peoples of East Asia" from the domination of the white man. And what chance for survival in Korea, in Manchuria, or in Formosa would an Aguinaldo, a Ghandi, or a Nehru have had?

When we have driven these Japanese "liberators" out of the 7,000 islands, the Filipino people will be in no condition to accept independence immediately. Their principal cities and towns have been bombed and burned and looted. It is a certainty that their grain reserves will be almost nil. There will be no money left except totally unsecured Japanese military yen. The treasury of the Commonwealth will be empty, unless it is filled with American loans. The vengeful Japanese will undoubtedly wreck and plunder as they retire. There will be no merchant vessels left for interisland communication, nor will there be immediately available great Pacific liners and freighters to take Philippine tropical products to nations ready to import. In fact, there will be little for the islands to export for many months, perhaps for several years. Certainly the great American-owned sugar mills will be wrecked, as will the mills which press the coconut oil, and the hemp industry will be in ruins.

This hemp industry, largely centered around Davao on the island of Mindanao, will be a problem in itself. It is more than 90 per cent Japanese-owned, and the 20,000 Japanese civilians there proved, almost to a man, to be disloyal to this country and to the Philippine Commonwealth and eager fifth columnists for the invading Japanese. The Filipinos hated them even before this war was begun, and their continued residence in the Philippines will be almost impossible. Probably they, too, will have to follow the Japanese in Manchuria and in Korea on a long trek back to their homeland.

The Filipinos, in the day of liberation, will be better off than will the peoples of the temperate zones who will be freed from the yoke of Nazi tyranny. In the Philippines, even though the islands be largely ruined, there will be no winter and no cold and no acute fuel and shelter problems. Rice is a quick and frequent crop, bananas and other tropical fruits are to be had for the reaching out of a lazy hand, and cotton shorts for the men and mother-hubbard-like garments for the women will suffice for clothes. Indeed, that is all that most of the peasants have ever worn or needed, and the same is true of a vast majority of the villagers.

The prospect for these brave people is not bright. Although the Commonwealth Government, before the Japanese invasion, had committed itself to the carrying out of lavish public-welfare programs before the proposed coming of independence in 1946, little had actually been done except to make promises. Resettlement schemes to shift large populations from overcrowded areas, - where land rents were prohibitively high, to undeveloped districts were encountering serious difficulties. The owners of large estates were reluctant to split up their holdings, except at prohibitive prices.

Excellent plans had been drawn up to make cheap Government credit available to farmers who were being oppressed by moneylending landlords, but the plans had not been put into operation. Agricultural schools were in existence, but were not popular; most educated Filipinos consider labor on the land fit only for the coolie classes.and show marked preferences for becoming lawyers, politicians, doctors, or literati.

A revival of prosperity for the islands will be impossible unless their sugar, copra, coconut oil, tobacco, and hemp are again permitted entry to this country without tariff levies for many years to come. Domestic American producers of these commodities will probably renew their opposition to free trade with the Philippines.

After the great depression of a decade ago, when the American and European markets for tropical colonial products declined alarmingly, the various regimes of southeastern Asia became interested in developing industries. The Philippines showed a particular interest in these problems, faced as they were with coming independence and the cessation of free access to American markets for their raw materials. There was a marked development of mining in the islands. The Commonwealth Government began to encourage animal husbandry and diversified food production and talked of industrialization, but made little progress along that line. Which is probably all to the good, for had factories been built they would now be of use to the Japanese or would have been ruined during the bombings and conflagrations which accompanied the invasion.

It is difficult to envisage a return to the governmental system which existed in the Philippines before the outbreak of war. Local self-government had been introduced as long ago as 1901, and six years later an elected legislative assembly was installed. Following a rapid extension of the franchise to include all literate citizens more than twenty-one years of age, there began the hasty and ill-advised Filipinization of all Government services. This abruptly turned out of office hundreds of experienced Americans and in many cases resulted in handing important administrative posts over to untrained men. By 1934, when the Independence Act was passed, there were only a handful of Americans holding important offices.

At the time of the Japanese invasion the Commonwealth was governed by a President, a Vice-President, and a senate and lower house, all chosen by direct vote of the people. The Commonwealth Government controlled all national affairs except the American share of the defense of the islands, foreign affairs, immigration, tariffs, coinage, and currency. Over these matters the President of the United States retained the power of veto, as well as the power of intervention if the security of the Commonwealth regime, the constitution, or the Philippine obligations to this country were held to be in jeopardy.

In spite of the fact that the Philippine constitution was generally modeled after that of the United States, there was a more marked tendency in the islands in peacetime toward centralizing power in the hands of the President, Manuel Quezon, than there was in this country until the war was well under way. For at least three decades there had been no important opposition or minority party, and the existing regime had become self-perpetuating.

The Tydings-McDuffie Act, which established the Philippine Commonwealth and pledged the grant of independence in 1946, also specified a "re-examination" of the Philippine problem not later than 1944. But even though war was becoming a certainty during the latter half of 1941, neither the people of the islands nor our own Congress seemed aware of what was certain to occur or even to speculate on what effects a war in the Far East would have upon the future of the Filipino people.

At this writing it seems unlikely that the war will be ended by 1944, and it certainly will not be ended sufficiently in advance of that year to make an intelligent "re-examination" of the Philippine problem possible then. Indeed, it is well within the limits of probability that the war will not be victoriously ended for the United Nations before 1946, the very year set for granting the islands absolute independence.

It is now painfully obvious that the Filipinos will not be ready for independence, politically, strategically, or economically, until at least a few years after the end of this war, and for the sake of the record the Tydings-McDuffie Act should be amended—preferably at the request of the Commonwealth's President, Manuel Quezon, and those members of his Government who are with him in the United States. The mere basic needs, such as reorganizing the Commonwealth Government, holding overdue elections, re-establishing law and order, training a new police and constabulary force, repairing ruined railways, highways, docks, and harbor works, and overcoming the epidemics which will be one of the ghastly heritages of the war —these things cannot be accomplished in months. It will

require years to re-establish the Commonwealth as a going
concern, and it may take years after the re-establishment
before the islands will be able to exist in prosperity without
free access to the American market for their products.

As long ago as 1931 the special position and protection
enjoyed by the Filipino people had raised their general
standard of living to a level estimated as 300 per cent higher
than any standard existing for native peoples on the
neighboring Asiatic mainland. One of the war's legacies
to China, Indo-China, Thailand, Burma, and possibly other
newly liberated countries will be extreme poverty and
probably even famine. The Filipino people will need, and
will deserve, our protection from lapsing into like conditions and from ruinous competition with hundreds of
millions of fellow Asiatics whose living standard, at least
for a few years, will be much lower than anything the
Filipinos have endured since just after the eviction of
Spanish misgovernment.

Before the war the United States bought more than
850,000 tons of Philippine sugar annually, and American
purchases have taken between 75 and 86 per cent of all
Philippine exports each year since 1926—all admitted to this
country duty-free. It will require at least a decade for the
islanders to establish a self-sustaining economy that will
assure them the maintenance of their accustomed living
standards when they are given absolute independence.

Idealism would probably prompt us to give them inde-

pendence as soon as the last Japanese soldiers have embarked
and sailed away. Realism will tell us that we should stay
in the islands, as the responsible governing authority, while
we repeat for at least a decade the kind of work we spent
four decades accomplishing before the invaders struck and
ruined forty years of achievement. But if we do this, we
shall welcome no renewal of denunciation and political
speechmaking misrepresenting our motives such as we
endured during the twenty years before December 7, 1941.
The vote-seeking politicos of the islands who throve on
false anti-American misrepresentations will do well to seek
other issues in the days of peace.

Remembering Bataan as a symbol, the United States will
be disposed to be softhearted toward the Philippines after
the war. But it will be necessary also to be tough-minded.
Common danger, common suffering, and a great common
effort have served to make both the Filipinos and ourselves
forget the old disputes, but they will arise in somewhat
changed form with the coming of peace. Then, above all,
will be the time we will not be able to afford to be gulled
by special pleaders, be they from the Philippine Islands,
from Korea, or from other parts of the Far East. And we
must be particularly alert against being beguiled by special
pleaders directly or secretly representing Japan.

When Mr. Francis Burton Harrison was Governor General, during Woodrow Wilson's administration, we gave
the Filipinos almost complete independence, and they mis-

used it scandalously. The Jones Bill, passed in 1916, made the Filipinization of the Government of the islands almost complete, and between then and 1921, when General Leonard Wood became Governor General, the administration of justice was disgraced, a business was made of politics, the National Bank was plundered, the Government attempted to invade the field of business with resulting scandals and losses of millions of pesos to the taxpayers, and public offices were crammed with incompetent and untrained appointees. The Act of Congress had, in other words, failed in seeking to impose the moral concepts of public service of the Western world upon the minds of Orientals.

The "bank scandal" became so serious that Philippine notes and drafts were refused by all banks in British colonies and in all parts of the Japanese Empire. By 1921 the National Bank, under Filipino mismanagement, was unable to meet obligations and was forced to ask creditor banks in Shanghai and elsewhere not to press for payments long overdue. The losses were tremendous. Under the Philippine law all municipal and provincial funds had to be deposited in the Philippine National Bank, and finally all trust funds, too, were acquired. A sum of $41,500,000, United States currency, held in this country for the conversion of the currency of the islands, was finally transferred to Manila in an attempt to bolster up the quaking structure. The Government's credit was impaired, the paper money of the

islands depreciated, and many branch managers were subjected to criminal charges.

It may be argued that no good is achieved by reviving
scandals more than two decades old, and that references to
the fiasco of 1916–21 will only offend a sensitive alien race
which, by aiding us in fighting the Japanese, proved its
bravery.

We never doubted the bravery of the Filipinos. They
fought armies from the United States with savage success
for two years after we took the islands from Spain. And
they would doubtless have fought the Japanese invaders
even if there had been no American forces in their islands
to aid them. If we are practical-minded about the Philippine
problem we must remember that they were fighting because
their homeland had been attacked, their cities bombed and
shelled, and their shores invaded. They hated and feared
the Japanese because they had known since midsummer of
1937 how the Japanese Army had treated the Chinese
people in occupied China and felt certain of like treatment
for themselves. The Filipinos were brave and welcome allies
for our forces, but they were not fighting primarily to help
the United States.

The Filipinos have long argued that it is their right to
misgovern themselves if they choose to do so. Indeed,
Manuel Quezon has never denied a saying widely attributed
to him, to the effect that "it would be better to be under
a government run like hell by the Filipinos than under one

run like heaven by the Americanos." They argue that certain administrations in our large cities, notably Chicago and New York, have been notoriously corrupt, and that we have no business criticizing them so long as we endure Tammanys, Huey Longs, and gangsterdom.

Political corruption will not be the only danger to be weighed. The collapse of the public-health service during the 1916–21 heyday of Filipino responsibility was as shocking as was the looting of the National Bank. In 1915 the deaths from smallpox in all the islands totaled only 276, but by 1919, with the health service completely staffed by Filipinos, they rose to more than 49,000. Deaths from cholera jumped from 820 in 1915 to 17,537 in 1919. By 1923, when the health service had been properly reorganized, deaths from smallpox totaled 5 and from cholera only 72.

We must not withdraw entirely from the Philippines until we have accomplished what we announced we were going to do—end illiteracy, educate the people in self-government, and establish them in security and prosperity.

The Philippine Islands are strung out along the east coast of Asia for a distance equivalent to that from our Canadian border to the Gulf of Mexico. They had less than 7,000,000 inhabitants when we took them from Spain. When Japan invaded, the population had risen to about 16,000,000, and it is estimated that they could support a population of 50,000,000. Impractical idealism must not be permitted to induce us to quit these islands when our work there is only half done.

The attitude of President Manuel Quezon toward the postwar settlement in the Philippines was fully set forth in a special interview which appeared in the New York *Times* on August 10, 1942. Mr. Quezon said:

Sometimes I have regretted that the Atlantic Charter is so named. Too many persons have fallen into the error of believing that it applies only to those who live beside the Atlantic Ocean.

But that is not the fact. In truth, the Atlantic Charter is a world-wide charter. It applies to the nations and peoples of all the world.

It is a charter for Europe and for America, for Africa and for Australia, and—let us be clear on this—it is a charter of freedom for the peoples of Asia and all the Far East.

The real test, Mr. Quezon declared, will come after victory has been achieved.

Then we shall be faced with the task of making good on our promises to ourselves.

We shall be called upon to make the post-war sacrifices that will take the principles of freedom out of a charter and put them into our every-day lives.

We shall embark on the gigantic task of creating a world without fear and without want, a world where all of us can live in freedom to speak and think and worship, a world where evil men can no longer break the peace.

That is the goal to which we dedicate ourselves, as we recall the signing of the Atlantic Charter. It is a goal which makes sense to Americans as well as to my countrymen on the Islands of the Philippines.

It is the language of the plain people of the Western Hemisphere and of the Eastern—indeed, it is the language, I think, of every one's heart who knows the dignity of man. It is the hope of peace and justice which makes the blood and sorrow of this war worth while.

CHAPTER VIII

France in the Orient

Frenchmen, in their days of opulence and power, were in the habit of referring to their great colonial possession of Indo-China as France's "balcony on the Pacific." A strange phrase, that, to describe a treasure house which might have become of inestimable value to the French Empire. Instead, for lack of attention, the props of the balcony rotted, and at the first strong push the whole structure crashed.

France today has neither balcony nor window on the Pacific. Indo-China is in the hands of the Japanese, and so are the French concession areas in Shanghai, Canton, Hankow, and Tientsin; and her groups of Pacific islands are nominally controlled by adherents of General De Gaulle, but are actually under the domination of the American naval, military, and air forces.

The French concessions in China will not be handed back to France. That is a certainty. They were profitable, but they were no credit to the French. In Shanghai, for instance, the French Concession was the center of gambling, prostitution, and the opium trade when China was trying to eradicate the drug evil. The police graft was colossal, and it was well known that most of the high French officials of the concession could, within a few years, retire to France with sizable fortunes which were certainly not saved from their salaries.

Both the Vichy and De Gaulle factions are in the habit of declaring with typical Gallic emphasis that after the war the French Empire must be restored in its entirety. But why? Just because France has suffered? That would be a fatuous excuse. Take the case of French Indo-China: the people there have suffered too. Suffered under rapacious French misgovernment. To hand them back to French domination after their Japanese oppressors have been driven out would be a criminal folly.

The term "colony," to most American readers, usually seems to imply a smallish scrap of territory. But the French colony of Indo-China is actually much larger than France. Here are the figures: Indo-China, 286,422 square miles; France, 212,659 square miles. And the population of Indo-China is about 24,000,000, or more than half the population of France itself.

The acquisition of Indo-China was managed piecemeal.

It began about 1860, with pressure being put upon the native kingdoms of Cambodia and Annam, but actual consolidation was not completed until 1907. When France and Germany went to war in 1939 the Union of Indo-China was made up of the colony of Cochin China, ruled by a French governor, the four protectorates of Cambodia, Annam, Laos, and Tonkin, and the port of Kwangchowan, leased from China. The administration of all these areas was centralized under a governor general. Laos, in theory, was ruled by a native prince, and Cambodia by a king, but these dignitaries, like the native heads of the protectorates of Tonkin and Annam, were actually subject to the dictation of French officials responsible only to the French governor general.

Although there was maintained a pretense of "indirect rule," and mandarins or local officials usually enforced the laws, the entire area was really ruled by the French and administered in the interests of France and French investors. Native elements were permitted to play only an ineffective and humiliating part in the real administration.

There is no real racial unity or nationalistic feeling in Indo-China. For many years the princes and kings of the region paid tribute to the Chinese emperors at Peking, but the Chinese Government of today has no wish to revive any ancient claims for suzerainty. The Annamites are the most up-and-doing group of the natives and almost outnumber all the other groups put together. Their culture is strongly related to that of China, whereas the culture of the Cambodians has been more largely influenced by India. In the interior there are primitive tribesmen, the Maos and the Laotians, who are almost untouched by life in the outside world.

The French put thousands of Annamites into uniform and tried to use them in Europe and elsewhere during the first World War. Although these peoples had for centuries been accustomed to the petty strife of tribes and principalities, they did not make good soldiers for the type of modern warfare of 1914–18 and could not stand up under heavy artillery or machine-gun fire, even with one French noncommissioned officer to every ten natives. After a while the Annamites were used principally for supply trains, to clean up the battlefields, and to bury the dead. Indo-China probably offers no reserve of military man power for the United Nations, even after they reconquer the area and have weapons enough to supply new native armies.

The rich, red alluvial soil of the deltas of the great Mekong and Red rivers supports most of the population with bountiful crops of rice. This grain had been made the staple food and principal export of Indo-China, with the result that the rice-growing regions are densely overpopulated, and the mountains and plateau districts have been neglected and are still mainly covered with jungle. The country has rich tin mines and considerable coal and zinc. Beginnings had been made in the cultivation of rubber groves, but the output did not bulk large in world trade, and most of the colony's exports, besides the rice, were pepper, maize, tea, hides, and dried fish. Imports were largely confined to cotton and silk fabrics, kerosene, and machinery.

French manufacturers, joining in the general plan of milking the country dry, managed to secure the enactment of high import tariffs against all goods not of French origin, but even so Japanese cotton goods were largely replacing cotton goods from France even before the Japanese took military possession. Indo-China was deliberately kept in the status of an agricultural colony, exporting raw materials and importing such quantities of French manufactured goods as the low standard of living of the millions of natives would permit them to purchase.

Even after the Japanese began their career of expansion in 1931 and talked openly of the necessity of moving southward, France did little to strengthen the defenses of this rich and vulnerable area and did nothing at all to build up an efficient and honest corps of colonial administrators. In spite of the near-by example of the United States in the Philippine Islands, the French made almost no attempt to cut down the high percentage of illiteracy and suppressed with heavy hand any incipient movements for autonomy or eventual independence.

French Indo-China was easily the worst example of the white man's imperialism to be found in all of East Asia and the southern seas. French policy was selfish and greedy, and was not offset by the fact that the French did not enforce a social color line against the natives and half-castes as did the British in most of their Empire, and as many of the Americans did in the Philippines.

The Filipinos, when the invasion came, fought shoulder to shoulder beside American soldiers and Marines because they felt they were fighting for their own future and eventual freedom. But the natives of French Indo-China had no reason to oppose the Japanese, except that they had heard of the atrocious manner in which Japanese soldiers treated the people of the occupied areas of China.

France could never restore the old order in Indo-China, even if the United States and Great Britain chose to forget the promises made in the Atlantic Charter. The United Nations will be bitterly disappointed if they consider the native populations of southeastern Asia and of the East Indies as a potential source of man power to help defeat the Japanese in the final stages of the war. J. M. Elizalde, the Philippine Resident Commissioner in Washington, summarized the situation truthfully and cleverly when he declared:

I frequently hear it said that in this war one fifth of the population of the world supports the Axis and the remaining four fifths is behind the United Nations. But is this true? I think we could more safely say that this war matches one fifth of the world against just another fifth. The remaining three fifths have no acute interest in the war. In Asia there is a great mass of colonial subjects who today merely stand on the side lines. And if they have nothing better to hope for in the future than the brand of imperialism they have known in the past, I for one can understand their reluctance to side wholeheartedly with the United Nations.

Unhappily there have been issued several official British statements pledging the restoration of French sovereignty in Indo-China, and even more unhappily on April 13, 1942, the American Government issued a note making a similar pledge. If, after a United Nations victory, whatever government may succeed the Vichy regime is permitted to send a new army of occupation to French Indo-China, and if France is permitted to resume exploitation of the 24,000,000 inhabitants of that country, it will be an outrageous betrayal of the letter and spirit of the Atlantic Charter.

Even if the French people were to have the vision and the will to try to prepare Indo-China for self-government, France will emerge from the war so shattered and so impoverished that she would be unable to carry on any educational campaign similar to that which the United States conducted in the Philippines for four decades.

Here, clearly, is a case similar to that of Korea. An international authority of some kind will have to be set up to guard Indo-China during a long period of political tutelage and to guide the ignorant millions into developing something akin to economic and political stability. France might plead with justice for a large representation on the Indo-China commission or guardianship organization, but if she is given a clear majority of the administrative personnel there will almost inevitably be a return to the ways of greed, corruption, and indifference there which were such a blot on the white man's record in the Far East. In the past in the administration of Indo-China the French had only two real interests, and those were France and their own pocketbooks.

China will have a vital interest in the future of Indo-China and also in the future of Burma. Before the Japanese seized the former French colony, southwest China looked to the Indo-China harbor of Haiphong as a port, and the railway from Haiphong to Kunming was China's "life line" in the interval between the time she lost all her own important seaports and the date when the Burma Road was completed. China will look to Haiphong again in the future as an outlet to the South China Sea and to Rangoon as an outlet westward toward the Indian Ocean, and will therefore be entitled to an important voice in whatever form of authority is set up to administer these two areas.

Just how Washington and London are going to get around their promises concerning the restoration of French sovereignty over Indo-China is not now clear. At best they will have to squirm unbecomingly and say that by their pledges they merely meant to signify that neither the United

States nor Britain intended to seize any former French territory for their own uses or expansions.

Even the conservative London *Economist*, long regarded as the mouthpiece of British finance, published a striking editorial a few weeks after the surrender of Singapore, calling for the announcement of a "Colonial Charter" in order that the natives of various British colonies who are politically conscious might know what they could expect to gain from a British victory. A fortnight later the *Economist* again took up this theme, declaring:

> There can be no return to the old system once the Japanese have been defeated. . . . The need is for entirely new principles—or rather, the consistent application of principles to which lip service has long been paid. For the colonies—Malaya, Indo-China and Netherlands India—there can be only one goal, the creation of independent nations linked economically, socially and culturally with the old mother-country, but learning to stand firmly on their own feet.

It is doubtful if the natives of Indo-Chino will have any desire for continuing any links with what the London journal calls "the old mother-country." The economic ties that existed under the French colonial system were all in favor of France. Socially there were practically no ties, and culturally there were none which the Annamites or Cambodians would care to revive or continue.

In the early spring of 1940, fearing a French debacle in

Europe and dismayed with the signs of dry rot evident in the administration of the French Concession at Shanghai, I made a survey trip through French Indo-China. To my amazement I found only about 25,000 Frenchmen in that great colony, and this total included military and naval men and civilians. French naval representation was pitifully weak, land forces were scarcely adequate to preserve local order, and even anti-aircraft equipment was not sufficient to give minimum protection to harbors and airfields.

Then, in May, came the collapse of France in Europe, and Japan was soon on the march southward. First the French-owned railway running from Haiphong to Kunming was forced to cease handling any cargo that could remotely be classed as war supplies for China. Movements of freight trucks on the roads running into Yunnan were limited to twenty a day, under Japanese pressure. Then Japan insisted on stationing "inspectors" along that portion of the railway which lies in Indo-China.

Border hostilities, for which Tokyo attempted to disavow all responsibility, brought disaster to the French. General Ando, the Japanese commander who then controlled the Nanning area in southeastern Kwangsi Province, had moved to the Indo-China border and attacked the French. A Japanese airman bombed Haiphong, and Tokyo said the usual "So sorry" and explained that the aviator had been actuated solely by "personal enthusiasm." The Japanese came out of this brush with control of Haiphong harbor, control of the railway as far as China's border, and five airfields in northern French Indo-China at the disposal of their military planes.

Then, in the summer of 1941, by an infamous agreement made with the Pétain regime in Vichy, Japan was granted the right of military occupation of southern French Indo-China. This gave her airmen fine landing fields within 400 miles of Singapore and gave her navy and transports bases at Saigon and Cam Ranh Bay. From then until December 7 Japan was busy using French territory for preparations for her ultimate onslaught upon the Philippines, Singapore, and the Netherlands East Indies.

Vichy could probably do nothing except yield to Japan's commands, but there was much that the French in Indo-China might have done between May of 1940 and the time of the actual Japanese occupation. Holland fell in May 1940, but the Dutch in the East Indies did not sit in complacent lethargy and wait for the Japanese to disembark without firing a shot.

Today the Frenchmen who are trapped in the ruins of their balcony on the Pacific are having a grim time of it. They are now in the hopeless position not only of being ruled by the Japanese, but of being completely surrounded by conquered countries, except for jungled Yunnan, and therefore being unable to escape to lands controlled by allies of the Fighting French forces.

The money they amassed so greedily is worthless today

—the Indo-China piaster is linked to the Japanese yen and when the crash comes will be worth even less than the French franc. Their merchant fleet of the Far East has been seized by the conquerors and will be either outworn or destroyed before the war is ended.

Today the rubber, tin, rice, and sugar which Indo-China produces all help the Japanese to fight the nations upon whose victory depends the future freedom of their French homeland, and the French in the conquered colony face the bitter necessity of working and producing materials and commodities which aid the ally of Germany. Hordes of the lazy and corrupt French petty officials now subserviently obey the Japanese.

Yet there are French patriots in Indo-China, just as there are in occupied France. The Saigon-Hanoi railway has been dynamited several times, resulting in the wrecking of Japanese troop and munitions trains. Several Japanese ammunition dumps have been exploded during the night by bullets fired by Frenchmen who hate the invaders enough to risk sabotage. But the Frenchmen in Indo-China are few, and the natives are cowed and apathetic. They have no incentive for doing anything to help the French restore their own forms of oppression and maladministration.

Someday the armies of the United Nations will land at Indo-China ports, or march into Indo-China from Burma, from China, from Malaya and Thailand. When that day comes they will receive a hostile and suspicious greeting from the 24,000,000 natives if those natives believe the victors are arriving in order to restore French rule. When the armies of the United Nations get to Indo-China they should arrive not only as liberators from the tyranny of the Japanese but as known heralds of a new and better day for Indo-China, and certainly not as conquerors with no motive other than to hand the inhabitants over to the old thraldom.

The people of Indo-China should be told, and told now, what a United Nations victory will mean for them. We should make them such specific promises of ultimate freedom that they would no longer remain merely disinterested spectators of the war, seeing no hope for themselves no matter what the outcome may be.

CHAPTER IX

Thailand for the Thais

It was the territorial rivalries of Great Britain and France which permitted Siam to survive as an independent nation. Each realized that a neutral buffer state between Malaya and Indo-China would have a distinct value to imperialism in southeast Asia, and therefore the Siamese escaped the fate of the peoples of the Malay Peninsula and of the Cambodians and Annamites. They survived not because of their own strength or wisdom but because of European rivalries.

What France and Britain achieved was the creation of a political and military vacuum. Japan sensed this fact, and a decade ago began making preparations to fill the empty space. Today French Saigon and British Singapore are both in the hands of the Japanese.

The Siamese boast of their ancient dynasty, but in reality it is no more ancient than those of nearly a score of weak kingdoms, principalities, and sultanates scattered over the vast areas where the Malay strain predominates. The Siamese have no real devotion to their dynasty and protested not at all at a palace revolution which put power into the hands of a profascist group, leaving the boy king, then being educated in Europe, as a mere figurehead.

When the absolute monarchy was abolished in 1932 an elaborate paper constitution was drawn up providing for a constitutional monarchy somewhat like that of Great Britain, but the paper constitution has never been given a chance to work. In theory, the king or his regent was supposed to exercise executive power and to determine policy, acting in conjunction with a national assembly, half of the members of which he appointed and half of which were supposed to be elected by popular ballot. In practice the national assembly has become merely a tool of a small group of ambitious politicians and military leaders who, within their own circle, have contended against one another for power. Finally the Army group became predominant. The people of Siam were either illiterate and uninformed or indifferent and apathetic to what was going on in Bangkok, the capital.

During the decade since the palace revolution Britain and France have paid little heed to the growth of nationalistic sentiment on the part of Siamese leaders. Their interest was focused on the drama of Hitler's rise to power and Germany's expansion. With half-hearted attention they agreed to the surrender of many special treaty privileges in Siam, although the rise of a politically conscious and nationalistic group in the midst of this great colonial area of southeast Asia was viewed with some alarm.

In 1939, encouraged by the Japanese and aping Japan's slogan of "Asia for the Asiatics," the fascist leaders of Siam changed the country's name to Thailand, or "Land of the Free," and proclaimed their innate anti-foreignism by adopting the slogan of "Thailand for the Thais." This was an astute move on the part of the ruling clique, for it brought them support from the millions of illiterate and hitherto indifferent rice-growing peasants, who interpreted the slogan as permission to persecute the hated Chinese immigrants.

Thailand is no small principality. The area is a little more than 200,000 square miles, and this means it is nearly as large as France in Europe and only 14,000 square miles smaller than Germany and Austria combined. The population is about 14,000,000, but by no means all these people are Siamese, or Thais.

Thailand's statistics are vague, but the number of Chinese in the country is known to exceed 2,500,000 and is believed to be near 4,000,000. In Thailand the Chinese are not laborers and coolies as they are in many of the areas to which they have migrated by the millions. Instead they have become the merchants, the middlemen, the money-lenders of the country. The average native is lazy and is not thrifty, so the industrious and saving Chinese have finally dominated much of the commercial life of the country. Naturally the people of Thailand resented this situation.

When the present controlling group of militarists and politicians came to power, they singled out the Chinese for persecution and plunder. No racial group has been as badly treated in modern times, with the single exception of the Jews under the Nazis in Germany and Austria. Restrictive and even confiscatory laws were passed. In fact, there was actual declared emulation of the German treatment of the Jews, and one Cabinet member declared publicly that Thailand should treat the Chinese just as Hitler had treated the descendants of the children of Israel.

Many classes of business controlled by the Chinese were nationalized or made Government monopolies by decrees issued by the Cabinet and rubber-stamped with approval by the national assembly. China, first engaged in civil war and then fighting for her life against the Japanese, could give no protection to the several millions of her citizens who were being thus abused.

Here was a situation entirely to Japan's liking, and Tokyo soon began cultivating the good will of Bangkok. Military missions, naval missions, cultural missions, and trade delegations shuttled back and forth between the two capitals. The Japanese encouraged the anti-foreignism of the Thailanders and adroitly channeled it against both the Chinese and the whites. Japan built light naval vessels for Thailand and cajoled the clique in Bangkok, which was ignorantly and ineptly playing at statecraft, to give to Japanese various concessions and monopolies which had been forcibly taken away from Chinese, Europeans, or Americans. The staff of the Japanese legation was increased enormously as the number of military and naval attachés was doubled and doubled again.

Among other special concessions which Japan obtained was the granting of a monopoly for refining oil. A costly refinery was built on the outskirts of Bangkok, and a staff of more than 200 experts arrived from Japan to operate the plant. The Dutch, the British, and the Americans, who then controlled the oil fields of Borneo and Sumatra, laughed in their sleeves, for the Japanese were denied ample supplies of crude oil on various pretexts, and the great refinery stood idle.

But now it is the turn of the crafty Japanese to laugh over this transaction. The huge refineries in the East Indies belonging to the white men were all destroyed when the scorched-earth policy was put into effect before the oil fields and ports were surrendered to the Japanese. But Japan had the big refinery at Bangkok, comparatively near by, ready to begin operations as soon as she got the wells flowing again.

So it was with high-octane gasoline. The Government of Thailand, building up a small air force, bought aviation gasoline in quantities far in excess of its own needs and stored this precious fuel at considerable expense. It was handily ready and waiting when Japan marched into Thailand in December 1941, and no doubt filled the tanks of the Japanese planes which bombed Singapore.

Japan also sent military engineers to help Thailand lay out air bases—bases from which Japanese bombers later raided Singapore, Penang, and Rangoon—and, besides helping to train Siamese military aviators, sold fifty bombing planes to the Bangkok regime and ostentatiously made Thailand a gift of ten more just after the United States Government stopped a shipment of ten American-made planes at Manila on the plea that they were needed by our own forces. That consignment was the last shipment of a total of one hundred American planes sold to Thailand. No doubt the other ninety were used to bomb the British and the Dutch, and possibly some of them assisted in raids on the Philippines.

Viewed in retrospect, it becomes evident that Japan's policy was extremely shrewd and that her generals were farseeing and astute while the democracies were blind, negligent, and so self-confident that they lacked even the intuition to be alarmed at the methods of Japan's gradual expansion southward, an expansion in which she was never opposed but was actively aided by the Thailand ruling clique.

The Japanese occupied Hainan Island and then the Paracels. They moved on southward and made the Spratly group into a submarine and seaplane base. They gained the

use of Indo-China's northern air bases, railways, and high-
ways. They made important dispositions in Thailand with-
out technically violating the sovereignty of that country.
And then, by a clever stroke, they further weakened the
French in Indo-China, after Hitler's armies had conquered
France, by inciting Thailand to open hostilities against the
French, advising them upon their strategy and furnishing
substantial credits to help finance the campaign.

This side-show war was a sanguinary affair but aroused
little interest outside southeast Asia because of the overwhelming importance of events developing in Europe late
in 1940. Thailand, with considerable justice, demanded
what was called "the redressing of ancient wrongs," including a new frontier to be drawn at the expense of Cambodia
and the cession of important islands in the Mekong River.
Historically the Thai claims were sound. The French rejected the demands, and for a time real hostilities were
carried on with modern artillery, bombing planes, and even
tanks. The Thais were victorious, and eventually an armistice was signed aboard a Japanese cruiser. The final peace
parleys were held in Tokyo, which helped to give Japan
prestige and in the eyes of millions of Asiatics seemed to
confirm her claim to being the arbiter and stabilizer of East
Asia.

This conflict not only increased Japan's hold upon Thailand but also weakened the French, who used up a considerable part of their reserves of munitions and were unable to

replenish their stocks because France in Europe could send them nothing. This simplified Japan's plans for occupying French Indo-China, which was accomplished without bloodshed in midsummer of 1941.

It was not until this occupation took place that the United States, Britain, and the Netherlands took positive retaliatory action by freezing Japanese assets and credits and suspending all trade with the Japanese Empire. Japan then found her trade restricted to Korea, Manchuria, occupied China, French Indo-China, and Thailand. From no other parts of the world could she obtain essential imports; to no other parts of the world could she sell her silk or other exports. It was impossible for her to replenish her oil supplies.

Prince Konoye's third Cabinet was ousted, the Army and Navy took charge, and the high command began formulating detailed plans for the raid upon Pearl Harbor, while the Foreign Office deceptively continued negotiations and finally sent Saburo Kurusu to Washington to "work for peace." During this period Japanese aircraft carriers and submarines, sailing under sealed orders, gathered around Hawaii and the Philippines for the kill. At the same time immense convoys of transports were steaming southward to attack the Philippines, land in Thailand, and assault the east coast of the Malay Peninsula. Thailand and French Indo-China, vague areas considered unimportant by most Americans, had played their part in preparation for an assault upon the democracies which was to be so successful that it would drive the white man out of East Asia and out of the Indonesian Archipelago in little more than ninety days.

Until the palace revolution of 1932 most of Thailand's exports consisted of rice and teak and went to what in the Orient are called "the Western nations." Europe and America held most of the country's foreign debt, and the king had surrounded himself with many advisers from the West, but did little to follow their sound advice.

This whole picture changed after the revolution, and particularly after the influence of Japan became important. The Government established wholesale and even retail agencies, agricultural co-operatives and savings banks for the peasants, and at the same time began engaging in manufacturing and other industrial enterprises. Strict new immigration laws were enacted to check the further influx of Chinese. By various confiscatory measures Chinese control of the developing tin and rubber industries was broken, although the Chinese who had tapped these hitherto undeveloped sources of wealth were efficient operators who had learned how to run mines and plantations by experience in Malaya or in Java. Rice milling became an important industry under Government control, and in addition to the rice and teak exports there was a growing foreign trade in copra, coconut oil, tin, rubber, tobacco, pepper, and cotton.

In 1933 Japanese imports were unimportant in quantity

and in value. Between 1934 and 1940 imports of Japanese-made cotton goods more than tripled, and by the close of 1940 imports of goods of all kinds from Japan greatly exceeded the combined imports from all other countries.

During this period a strutting, pugnacious type of man became Premier and gradually gathered to himself the portfolios of Foreign Minister and Minister for Defense, to which he later added the title of commander in chief of the Army, Navy, and Air Force. His name is Luang Bipul Songgram, and while he was playing into Japan's hands in secret he pretended to be merely an observant critic of Japan's policy on the Asiatic mainland.

"I am watching the development of the Greater East Asia Co-prosperity sphere with interested attention," he told me late in November 1940.

Less than a month later, on December 5, Bangkok and Tokyo made a joint announcement admitting that a "treaty of amity" had been negotiated and signed in secret. The document itself was never made public, but the announcements said it provided that for the next five years the two Governments would "consult on all questions of mutual interest, and respect each other's territorial integrity."

When Japan went to war in the Pacific in 1941 it was announced that the Thai armies resisted invasion "for one hour" and then surrendered at seven in the morning on December 8. This "resistance" was probably nothing more than a ruse for the sake of the record. Certainly Thai troops invaded Burma, and Thai planes helped to bomb Rangoon. And Thailand eventually declared war against the United States and Britain.

Before less than a year had elapsed the ruling group in Bangkok were thoroughly sick of their bargain, and the bulk of the population were filled with a sullen resentment against the oppressive measures enforced by the Japanese military.

Under the co-prosperity sphere, as Japan interprets it, the Thais are entirely unfit for self-government, as are the Filipinos. Officials and other *évacués* reaching the United States and Europe from the Far East brought word that the Japanese military had announced in Manila that the Filipino people must "be weaned from pernicious ideas of American democracy" before they can be given autonomy within Japan's planned new empire, and that the Thais "are too ignorant, too treacherous, and too superstitious" to be permitted to run their own affairs. In the matter of treachery they certainly had capable teachers!

Thailand now awaits deliverance from a military rule as harsh and as arrogant as that under which the Koreans have suffered for nearly forty years. Repatriated missionaries declare that Thai patriots, professors, students, writers, and speakers are subjected to arbitrary arrest by Japanese civilian police, and that when they are jailed they vanish. Communication with their families, friends, or attorneys is not permitted.

Japanese "observers" now direct the activities and meetings of all social and religious organizations. Freedom of speech is only a memory, and the Thai press has been suppressed. Even the peasants plant what their Japanese military masters order them to raise, and the Japanese Army has first call on all food crops, at its own price. Furthermore the unsecured Japanese military yen are used for all purchases, and the Japanese and Thai armies are paid in this worthless paper money.

Bangkok and other Thailand cities were heavily damaged, with accompanying large casualty lists, when the American "Flying Tigers" and British planes could still reach them in flights from air bases in Burma, and the native people know that they must suffer more devastation of that kind before they are finally freed of the presence of the now hated Japanese.

Thailand will present a grave problem to the peacemakers. The country willfully co-operated with our Japanese enemies, but the masses of the people were not responsible for the personnel or the policies of the handful of men who seized power and allied themselves with the Japanese. In fact, the masses of the people were too illiterate to know or care what was going on.

It would be folly to put the boy king on the throne again at the end of the war, and yet the Thais are obviously neither trained nor educated for any kind of self-governing democratic regime. They have enough of the spirit of nationalism, however, to resent bitterly the merging of their country into a conglomerate state made up of Thailand, Indo-China, and Malaya. Moreover the Thais are hated and even scorned by some of their neighbors. The Malays south of them on the peninsula indulged in hearty, ribald laughter when the slogan "Thailand for the Thais" was adopted at Bangkok, for in the Malay language the word "thai" signifies an unprintable epithet, and the Malays maliciously declared that the Thailanders had named themselves very fittingly. Seemingly Thailand offers another instance of a huge and very rich area inhabited by a backward people who will have to undergo a long period of political tutelage and guardianship under some kind of international authority and protection until they can be educated sufficiently to preserve freedom when it is given to them.

Thailand of the future will offer one of the great testing grounds in the Far East for the just treatment of racial minorities. The future of the several millions of Chinese in the country will present serious problems for whatever administration may be set up. In the past the Chinese were not permitted to become really loyal Thailanders, for they were hated and abused by the natives of the country. In the future, if they are given the chance and will consent to become loyal citizens instead of remaining predominantly loyal to China, one of the most difficult phases of the racial minority problem will be on the way to solution.

The peoples of southeast Asia have certain similarities

and common cultural backgrounds. It is possible that within a generation they might coalesce and form a really important national group. But there is just as much likelihood that if they are not wisely led the whole vast area south of China's border may develop into the Oriental equivalent to the Balkans.

CHAPTER X

What of the Dutch?

In the long view of history, when the dead of this war have been forgotten and the ruined cities rebuilt, it will probably be judged that the main achievement of the Japanese aggression in East Asia was to hasten and force a searching examination of the merits and methods of Western imperialism in the Far East.

Certainly the domestic and international status of some 450,000,000 Chinese will, in the end, have been greatly benefited as a result of the long war against Japan. Some solution of the problem of the 388,000,000 inhabitants of India will have been accelerated. Next, in point of numbers, will be the 70,000,000 inhabitants of the Netherlands East Indies, who must also have a new status with the coming of peace.

The Dutch are a courageous and stubborn people. They have fought magnificently in this war, have shown themselves amenable to teamwork, and have maintained a high morale both in conquered Holland and in those parts of the world where the remnants of their Army, Navy, and Air Force still have liberty of action. Their by no means inconsiderable merchant marine has also carried on gloriously in spite of shocking losses from submarine and airplane attack. So much for the courage of the Netherlanders.

But their stubbornness is likely to cause trouble for the United Nations when the time comes for arranging the peace, for the Dutch are determined to maintain sovereignty over the Netherlands East Indies. Yet a large number of Indonesians seek an end to Dutch rule and will feel that they have been betrayed if their faith in the Atlantic Charter and its promises proves to have been unjustified.

Added to the difficulties of the situation is the fact that the native inhabitants of the Netherlands East Indies would not be qualified for partial self-government, actual autonomy, or independence even if Holland were to grant them the choice of these three modes of living.

The uncompromising attitude of the Nationalist leaders, most of whom are Javanese and who were gathering a rapidly growing following before Japan struck southward, is that it is bitterly unjust to have 70,000,000 people ruled and commercially exploited by a nation of 8,000,000 people whose homeland is half the world away. Holland, they point out, is a tiny country with an area of only 13,481 square miles, while the East Indies have a land and water area as large as the United States, and a land area of 735,000 square miles, or almost five times the size of the State of California.

In further support of their arguments against continuing under Dutch rule, the Javanese Nationalists point out that Holland could never be strong enough to assure her East Indies Empire of real protection, and they prove their case by pointing to the rapidity with which Japan overran the archipelago.

Their group of islands, the Indonesians point out, are strung along north and south of the Equator for about 3,600 miles from east to west, and about 1,800 miles from north to south. In the days of marine supremacy these islands divided the Pacific and Indian oceans, but in the coming days of air supremacy they will be steppingstones connecting those two oceans.

Still another argument of the separatists is that although there are about 3,000,000 Christians and 1,000,000 Buddhists in the islands, the vast majority of the population are Mohammedans and therefore should not be ruled by a Christian nation. This argument has the least merit of any, for the Dutch have never interfered with religion in the East Indies, and there is no justification for trying to make it a political issue.

The Netherlands subscribed to the Atlantic Charter by signing the joint declaration of the United Nations early in January 1942, and the clause in that charter which means most to the Indonesians is this: "They respect the right of all peoples to choose the form of government under which they will live."

In spite of this pledge, leaders of the Netherlands have made it unmistakably plain that they have no intention of relinquishing any degree of sovereignty over any part of their Empire, whether it be in the Far East, in the Caribbean, or in South America. Addressing a joint session of Congress in Washington on August 6, 1942, Queen Wilhelmina referred to the East Indies in the following blunt manner:

Throughout my reign, the development of democracy and progress in the Netherlands Indies has been our constant policy.

Under Netherlands stewardship, a great number of peoples and tribes are being systematically merged into one harmonious community, in which all these elements, the Indonesians in their rich variety of religions, languages, arts and customary laws, the Chinese, the Arabs, and the Westerners, feel equally at home.

Careful consideration has constantly been given to the particular characteristics and needs of the peoples concerned.

Confronted as we found ourselves by highly developed forms of civilization to which the population is deeply attached, we strove not to uproot these, but to promote their adaptation to the exigencies of the modern world.

The voluntary cooperation in mutual respect and toleration

between the people of Oriental and Western stock towards full partnership in government on a basis. of equality has been proved possible and successful.

Increasing self-government, keeping pace with the rapidly broadening enlightenment and education of the native population, has been enacted ever since the beginning of this century and especially since the revision. of the Constitution in 1925.

This steady and progressive development received new emphasis and momentum by my announcement last year that after the war the place of the overseas territories in the framework of the kingdom and the constitution of those territories will be the subject of a conference in which all parts of the kingdom are to be fully represented.

Consultations on this subject were already proceeding in the Netherlands Indies when the Japanese invasion temporarily interrupted their promising course.

The preparation of the conference is none the less being actively continued, but in accordance with sound democratic principle no final decision will be taken without the cooperation of the people, once they are free again.

Later in her address, in order to leave no doubt of her meaning, Her Majesty declared:

We want nothing that does not belong to us.

We want to resume our place as an independent nation on the fringe of the Atlantic, on the dividing line of the Pacific and Indian oceans, and to remain your good neighbor in the Caribbean Sea, and we accept the responsibilities resulting from that situation.

Before Queen Wilhelmina came to visit the United States her ambassador in Washington, Dr. Alexander Loudon, speaking at a conference of governors at Asheville, North Carolina, on June 22 also made his country's intentions clear. He said, in part:

I would like to add a few words about the Netherlands East Indies. The world has given that part of our kingdom the adjectives of "fabulously wealthy." An honorable qualification indeed—if used with recognition of the fact that the wealth of the Netherlands East Indies is almost entirely due to Dutch stewardship, Dutch enterprise, Dutch capital, and Dutch civilization. It gives us, it seems to me, an unquestionable title to our heritage in Asia. . . .

Yes, indeed, the Netherlands East Indies is not a colony, but an integral part of the kingdom.

The natives of the East Indies have few burning grievances against the Dutch. They freely admit that they have been better off and more considerately treated than have any peoples of colonial status except the Filipinos since the United States took the Philippine Islands from Spain.

The announcement from London by the exiled Netherlands Government that after the war the East Indies would occupy a position within the Empire precisely equal and similar to the position of Holland itself aroused no enthusiasm in Java. The Indonesians complained that they were subject to rigid economic exploitation, that there was one

set of laws for whites and the half-castes and another for
the natives. They admitted all the splendid work of development, crop improvement, sanitation, and the beginnings
of education that the Dutch had conferred upon them.
They acknowledged that many native rulers had been left
at the heads of their states. They conceded that they were
subjected to few social disabilities and that all half-castes
were ranked as "whites" both socially and officially.

But—and they always returned doggedly to this summary
of their position—they simply do not want to feel that they
belong to any alien people far overseas. They want to feel
that they belong to themselves and have the human right
of working out their own collective destiny.

A collective destiny will be a difficult thing for them
to achieve. One of the first difficulties is the fact that there
are more than 200 dialects in the islands. The half-naked
savage of the Borneo jungles differs as night from day from
the cultured Javanese of Batavia. The Balinese differ, too.
Moreover, although the Netherlands controls most of the
islands of the rich archipelago, Borneo is or was cut into
three parts—Dutch Borneo, British North Borneo, and Sara-
wak, the native state with a white ruler, the third Rajah
Brooke. The island of Timor is not all Dutch; half of it
belongs to Portugal. Only half of New Guinea is Netherlands territory. The other half is Australian, or held by
Australia under mandate.

The Dutch have tried to Javanize the rest of the islands,

with considerable success, although the natives of Celebes and of New Guinea are basically as different from the people of Java as Italians are different from Danes. When the Nationalists demand that the islanders be given the right to work out their own "collective destiny," they neglect to give credit to the Dutch for having created such unity as now exists amongst the islanders.

The great bulk of the 70,000,000 people of the islands are illiterate and entirely devoid of political training. The processes of education and modernization have not gone far enough for the Indonesians to take over and complete the gigantic task that lies ahead.

Clearly there would be no justification for booting out the Dutch, nor will there be any justification for telling the Indonesians at the end of the war that the Atlantic Charter promises do not apply to them. If a nation is to be created in the East Indies, the Dutch are best fitted by tradition and experience to carry on the job. But will they consent to do it? Or will they take over the task, believing that they can perform the work so well and so justly that when the education and training of these 70,000,000 people have been completed they will wish to remain an integral and equal part of the Netherlands Empire?

That portion of the Atlantic Charter which promises all nations, victors and vanquished alike, "access, on equal terms, to the trade and to the raw materials of the world" will end the economic advantage of possession of colonies.

In the past the lure of material advantage and access to wealth was the main urge to colonial expansion, but if the Atlantic Charter is carried out with fidelity the possession of colonies will no longer assure exclusive profits.

The Dutch have been in the Indies for more than three centuries. They went there first for trade—particularly trade in spices. As their commerce expanded, political penetration followed naturally. The people were mild and amiable. Most of them were small-scale farmers or lived in villages, and their interests did not extend more than a few miles from their homes. They had no needs which could not be supplied locally.

From about 1880 until the great depression of a decade ago the Netherlands followed a genuine open-door policy in the East Indies. Citizens of other nations could invest and trade under the same laws and regulations as could Hollanders. This resulted in a great influx of foreign capital, particularly that of British and American corporations, which made large profits from oil fields, tin mines, rubber plantations. The national income soared, but because of the excellent public-health work of the Dutch the native birth rate increased with tremendous rapidity while the death rate was being lowered. The population of the island of Java doubled in three decades, and that island alone has 40,000,000 inhabitants.

Great estates were founded, particularly for the production of rubber and quinine and kapok. These estates pro-

duced nothing used by the native population, but the existence of the estates created pay rolls at the same time that
they reduced food production and helped increase the cost
of living. Until after the depression there was little encouragement for the development of industries. Profits from the
vast foreign investments were drained away to pay share-
holders in Europe and America. The population, particularly that portion living in the cities or employed by the
great foreign-owned corporations, developed the needs and
tastes for goods manufactured abroad. Then imports, tariffs,
and industry became geared to benefit the mother country,
and the drainage of native wealth became greater year by
year.

These processes are not listed here as iniquities practiced
in the islands by the Dutch. They are processes naturally
inherent in the colonial system as it grew up under what
became known as Western imperialism. Colonies became
sources of raw-material supply, cheap-labor supply, and
markets for goods made in the factories of the governing
country.

With the coming of peace the Chinese and all the colonial
peoples of East Asia will want to cease being economic subjects as well as political subjects of other nations. They
will want to industrialize, to make the things they use, and
to make them cheaper than they can be made in America
or in Europe. They will begin to exploit their own man
power and also will try to found industries which can man-

ufacture their own raw products. They will try to end the period of economic slavery in which they have been merely producers of raw materials manufactured elsewhere.

Even before the Japanese began to move into southeast Asia and into the East Indies the pronouncements of the Atlantic Charter had started a great ferment in those far-off regions. How the pledges of that Roosevelt-Churchill pronouncement can be kept to the letter without ultimately impoverishing the Western nations and reducing the standard of living in the white man's countries is a problem not yet even nearing solution. But those promises must be kept, even if keeping them results in leveling down our own ideas of material well-being while we level up those of the Asiatic and Indonesian peoples. Between Yokohama and Suez there are roughly a billion Asiatics. They want to end bondage to overseas powers, they want equality, they want the promised four freedoms, and they want the profits from their own labor and products.

If they are denied these things, if they feel they have been deceived and betrayed, if the yellow and brown men band together against the whites, civilization will face a new peril in comparison to which the perils of this war will seem almost like safety.

In the East Indies the task of making good the promises of the Atlantic Charter must be entrusted to the wisdom of the people of the Netherlands. Even though their position and authority there will necessarily be subject to great changes, and their profits subjected to sharp decreases, it will be their task to reconcile the Indonesians to a period of tutelage to end with freedom of decision regarding their ultimate destiny. There is no other choice, except the risk of making the leaders of 70,000,000 people sullen, disappointed, and rebellious-minded.

CHAPTER XI

Princes in Malaya

THE RAJAHS and the Sultans have departed. Nine Malay kingdoms and principalities with fantastic names which clang like Malay temple gongs—Selangor and Kelantan, for instance—are occupied by the Japanese.

And the British kings of finance, princes of mining and industry, and the dunces of diplomacy and strategy—they are gone too. Besides holding the native principalities, the Japanese now occupy proud Penang, Malacca, and even "impregnable" Singapore. The Rajahs and the Sultans saved at least their jewels, and in some cases their harems. But the British who really ruled Malaya were not able to save their pride or even their self-respect, although it is reported that most of them saved their shirts—the stuffed shirts, I mean.

It is doubtless wholesome to make confession of error of judgment and to admit an injustice of appraisal of the courage and fiber of a great people. I do that here and now. The error of judgment was that after the collapse of France and the evacuation of Dunkirk I was despairingly convinced that Great Britain could not endure a prolonged aerial blitzkrieg, that defeat was certain, and that the day of greatness of the British Empire had come to an end. These conclusions were reached with profound sorrow, for I had always ranked the British Empire as the greatest civilizing force the world has ever known.

These errors of judgment were occasioned by the fact that I had never lived or worked as a newspaperman in Britain and knew England and Scotland only as a tourist may know them. My judgment was based upon the type known as the "British colonial" as he lived and worked and played at diplomacy in the Far East. It was depressing to compare the forthright, able, vigorous descendants of Britons who lived in the great Dominions—Canada, Australia, New Zealand—with the Britons of today who were sent out to conduct imperial affairs in far parts of the world.

Hongkong was bad enough, but Singapore was worse. And it was dismaying to see high British diplomats who had proved themselves stupid and inept at their jobs in China and Japan being given key positions in wartime in vital areas like North Africa and Turkey. "If those are the best men Britain has to send out to represent imperial interests," I said to myself, "then even heaven cannot help the Empire."

But I was wrong. Chamberlain and most of his crowd were swept into limbo, Britain endured the terrible summer and autumn of 1940, and it became evident that tenacity and courage still existed in the British Isles. The people had not been weakened and softened by more than a century and a half of emigration of the most virile and daring of their sons or by the frightful slaughter of the first World War.

But there were few changes in Singapore and in Malaya as a whole. The few new men who were sent there to plan to meet the growing threat from Japan were unable to shake the hold upon power of the greedy, the lethargic, and the ignorant and self-satisfied clique who had long held the reins of power. As a result the Japanese overran the whole of the Malay Peninsula at a cost in lives and time much less than they had calculated, and Singapore was finally surrendered while 65,000 fighting men still had guns in their hands.

In the long view it is probably a good thing for the cause of world democracy that the "colonial British" were in Singapore and other far places. Grievous as is the loss of many outlying bastions of the British Empire, had the Singapore type stayed at home and been in charge of affairs in Great Britain, the war in Europe would possibly have been won by Hitler before the Japanese attacked Pearl Harbor.

For years there has been a noticeable difference in the

sort of Britisher who goes away from home "on his own" and a vast majority of the kind sent to distant parts of the Empire as officials or as representatives of great companies controlled by British capital. There seems to have been a dry rot at the top, and most of those sent are infinitely less able than the typical man who has gone "on his own." In general it may be said that the class from which the appointees are selected is, in enterprise and in intelligence, the inferior one.

The Britain that rallied so magnificently after Dunkirk did not merit losing the Malay Peninsula, but the British who were in control in Singapore and in Malaya deserved to be booted out. In some places, noticeably Penang, they did not wait to be booted out, but fled. And they can never go back at the end of the war under conditions resembling those which existed before the Japanese ejected them so ignominiously. Having acquired a strong Oriental consideration for "face," that particular type will probably not want to go back at all.

These criticisms are not directed against the fighting men who waged a losing battle—a retreating battle—from the beginning of the Japanese onslaught. Those men of famous English, Scottish, and Welsh regiments, of whole divisions of native volunteer troops from India, and of the Australian infantry fought magnificently. But the "higher ups" did not do so well. At Penang they left the harbor filled with undamaged ships for the Japanese to use along the west coast; they left the tin smelter unharmed, and thousands of ingots of smelted tin were on the docks. From Penang hundreds upon hundreds of civilian officials and businessmen fled secretly, giving their employees or servants a "holiday" and a few extra dollars to spend while they furtively packed.

In Singapore, the night of the first air raid, they did not black out the city until a quarter of an hour after the last Japanese bomb had been dropped. And this in spite of the fact that they knew Pearl Harbor and Hongkong and Manila had been attacked.

The men who will not want to go back and face the natives of Malaya are the men who would not tax their enormous rubber and tin profits more than an 8 per cent maximum; the men who could see no necessity for an income tax, who "faced the war" by continuing overeating, overdrinking, and mobbing the races; the men who would not deign to invite Australian soldiers to their homes and would not admit Australian officers to their clubs.

There are other men who, if they survive combat, will not want to go back to Singapore. These will include the experts who spent tens upon tens of millions of pounds making the Singapore naval base "impregnable," but pointed all the guns seaward; who made practically no provision for defending the base or Singapore Island from attack from the near-by mainland to the north; and who, in spite of the bitter lessons of Norway, Greece, and Crete, made almost no provision for anti-aircraft defense.

To these must be added the army engineers who said they had mined the mile-long causeway connecting Singapore Island with the mainland so that it would be "utterly destroyed" in case an enemy captured the north shore. The "utter destruction" was so inefficient that within twenty-four hours the Japanese had repaired the causeway and were sending trucks and guns and infantry pouring across.

Another class who will be reluctant to return will be those military pundits who insisted that no attackers could advance through the mainland jungles, that tanks could not cross the tropical marshes, and that Singapore could be made immune from attack from the north by the simple expedient of dynamiting the highways, railways, and bridges and felling some trees across the rights of way.

The British territories in Malaya covered an area of 52,000 square miles, which is slightly larger than the State of Alabama and a little less than one third the size of the State of California. Stamford Raffles, later Sir Stamford, obtained the first foothold for Great Britain at Singapore in 1819, when he arrived with half a dozen ships and leased part of the island from the Sultan of Johore. Five years later the whole island, only 217 square miles in extent, was bought outright for the East India Company. It was in 1824, too, that Britain and Holland settled their disputes in that part of the world, Holland relinquishing all claims on Malacca, which they had taken from the Portuguese,

and recognizing the Malay Peninsula as a "British sphere
of influence," while the British in turn recognized Dutch
sovereignty over the East Indies as we know them today.

For half a century Britain made no effort to expand her
position on the Malay Peninsula beyond what was known
as the Straits Settlements, which included Singapore, the
island of Penang which had been purchased from the Rajah
of Kedah, the adjoining mainland province of Wellesley,
and Malacca.

In 1874, however, irritated by continuing depredations
by Malay pirates, the occasional difficulties of British
traders in the interior, and Siamese political agitation
amongst the native state rulers, Britain began a long course
of political expansion which continued, largely at the expense of Siamese territorial pretensions, until 1909.

The Malay rulers of four native states, Selangor, Pahang,
Negri Sembilan, and Perak, formed a joint British protec-
torate in 1894 under the name of the Federated Malay
States. In addition there are five Unfederated Malay States—
Johore, Kelantan, Kedah, Trengganu, and Perlis. In the
Federated States, Britain stationed "Residents," and in the
Unfederated States was content with "Advisers." Actually
all nine native rulers were bound by treaty to follow the
advice of the Governor of the Straits Settlements, who was
also High Commissioner and representative of the King of
England. This loose form of administration was held to-
gether by the able and hard-working Malay Civil Service,

staffed by about two thirds British and one third Malays.

This odd conglomeration of territories and administrations, with a combined population of a little more than 5,000,000, was considered the richest area of its size in the world before it was conquered by the Japanese.

The Straits Settlements were largely occupied with shipping, imports and exports, and tin smelting. The Federated States experienced intensive modernized development of railways and highways, mining, agriculture, jungle clearing, and rubber culture. Johore, since it was closest to the island of Singapore, shared in this development, but the other four Unfederated States remained more primitive and had a lesser economic and political importance.

Dutch, British, and American money poured into the Malay Peninsula, which furnished more than half the world's production of tin and rubber. But the native Malays dislike regular work in mines, fields, or rubber groves, and consequently there was a correspondingly large importation of labor to match the importation of foreign capital. The imported labor came mostly from China and India but, as the riches of Malaya increased, the innate reluctance of the individual native to raise more food than he could himself consume resulted in Malaya's importing fully two thirds of its essential rice supply from Thailand.

Although the British long ago adopted a slogan of "Malaya for the Malayans," the importation of foreign labor had resulted by 1939 in a situation where more than half the population were Chinese and Indians and East Indians, and only about 47 per cent were Malays. Malaya had become an enormously wealthy reservoir for raw materials—mainly tin and rubber—not found in such abundance elsewhere in the world, and it boasted the world's highest per capita wealth. Actually, however, the average native was desperately poor. The wealth was amassed by the British, by European- and American-owned corporations, by the native rulers, and to a large and increasing extent by Chinese and Indian merchants, middlemen, and moneylenders.

In spite of the fact that a vast majority of the natives of Malaya remained barefooted, sarong-clad peasants living in thatched huts, there was almost no political dissatisfaction in the Malay States. The princes were rich and getting richer and thought they were safe as part of the ruling group of the British Empire. The word "protectorate" implied protection, and they thought they would get it. British rule was not oppressive, the sultans were not permitted to overtax their people, and native customs and religions were not subjected to interference.

There was no urge to unity or to nationalism in the Malay States. British control had brought order and stability, modern transportation, broadened education, efficient public-health services, a common and stable currency, and a suppression of piracy and brigandage.

There was little fifth-column activity in Malaya because

most of the natives were well content. The Chinese, as a class, were dissatisfied, but their discontent was based largely upon social grounds, and they did not help the Japanese because their loyalty was directed mainly toward Chungking. Even Chinese born in Singapore, who had never been to China, considered themselves Chinese citizens rather than British subjects, and their pride was hurt when their repeated offers of volunteer military service were rejected by the British authorities. Not until the situation of Singapore was hopeless did the British arm any of the Chinese who had long been eager to help defend the land in which they lived although they did not regard it as their homeland.

The tin mines of Malaya had been fought over for centuries, even before the Dutch and Portuguese battled at Malacca in 1641. A great city grew up on the island of Singapore about the year 1250, only to be destroyed by Javanese conquerors in 1365. Stamford Raffles and his men found the ruins of this city in 1819 when they began to clear away the vines and jungle growth from a hill close to the harbor.

By 1937, the last year of peace, Singapore was one of the world's greatest seaports, clearing more than 6,000 vessels aggregating more than 16,000,000 tons every year. Strategically, particularly before the perfection of the airplane as a war weapon, the importance of Singapore was tremendous, for it controlled the most direct route between the Pacific and the Indian oceans and the shortest route between Australia and New Zealand and Suez.

After the war it is probable that Malaya and most of southeast Asia will experience a severe economic depression. The tin mines have suffered destruction under the scorched-earth policy. Singapore and Penang will no longer have a monopoly in the smelting of tin ore; new Texas plants alone will be able to handle a large part of the tin requirements of the United States, using ores from Bolivia. Synthetic-rubber production in this country and the development of rubber in Brazil and elsewhere in this hemisphere will seriously reduce the Malayan income from rubber lands.

Since there is no urge to autonomy or independence in Malaya, Great Britain will probably be left to restore stability and government as she sees fit, but with the ferment for freedom spreading from India and from the Philippines it is improbable that the old native rulers can be reinstated in their positions of mock authority. And since the British were ignominiously defeated and driven out of Malaya by an army of Asiatics, their hold upon the Asiatic peoples of the peninsula can never again be really secure.

Unpalatable as the idea may be to the British, and unwelcome and startling as it may be to the average American, the peoples of southeast Asia are more likely to look to the United States than to Great Britain as the source of power and future security and social and economic justice.

Present strategic indications are that British man power,

ships, and planes will share with those of Soviet Russia the main burden of the task of defeating Germany, even though direct American participation in the battle for Europe will be large. The indications are, too, that American and Chinese man power and American ships and planes will play the leading part in the defeat of Japan. If this proves to be true to the end of the war, the prestige of the British will be further diminished in East Asia, and the prestige of Americans will be greatly enhanced, whether they or we like such an outcome or not.

CHAPTER XII

Anti-British Burma

To MOST AMERICANS Burma has always been a part of India, largely, probably, because Kipling's earlier poems and ballads had much to do with that one-time kingdom. Indeed Kipling's knowledge of Burma and its geography was vague too, as is evidenced in his "Mandalay," wherein he rhapsodizes over the impossible—the dawn coming up like thunder "outer China 'crost the Bay."

Actually the Burmese problem is entirely different from the problem of India. The only thing in common between the two countries is an anti-British bias. In the case of Burma this is further complicated by bitter anti-Indian hatred. One of the principal reasons for anti-British feeling in Burma is that British policy long ago made the fundamental error of attaching Burma to India. The separation was not officially made until 1937.

Until the last few years Burma was one of the most inaccessible regions in the world, except from the sea. Roads and railroads into Thailand were non-existent, and only mule trails led through the mountains into India. Then China built the Burma Road, and the railway from Rangoon through Mandalay and on to the Chinese border became a tremendous artery of trade—gasoline and war supplies for China going inland, and antimony, tungsten, tung oil, and other Chinese products coming seaward to the port of Rangoon.

Burma has an area of 261,610 square miles, which means that it is less than 1,000 square miles smaller than the State of Texas. The population is 15,000,000, of whom two thirds are the civilized but largely illiterate people of the lowlands, river valleys, and delta lands. The other 5,000,000 are the tribesmen of the Shan States and the Chin Hills—a mixture of Tibetan-Burman blood. They have been so much a law to themselves that their knowledge of the Central Government was slight.

A century and a quarter ago Burma was a warlike nation ruled by a powerful dynasty. The Burma of those days was inclined to be an "aggressor nation," but the thirst for conquest and expansion brought about three wars with Great Britain, running from 1824 until 1886. These wars were occasioned by Burmese preparations to invade northeast India and finally resulted in the dethronement of the monarchy and the annexation of Burma to India as a subsidiary province.

This attempt to merge two alien peoples was a profound mistake. Most of the people of India are Hindus or Moslems. The Burmese are of Mongolian, not Indian, derivation, and most of them are very devout Buddhists. Under British rule Indians immigrated into Burma in large numbers. They became prosperous merchants, bankers, and moneylenders, and early in this century the percentage of Burmese farms and rice plots mortgaged to the Indians was so large that it became an important political problem. Since 1931, foreclosures of these mortgages have led to serious anti-Indian rioting.

Burma was partitioned from India in 1937, and the establishment of an autonomous government was welcomed by the Burmese, who had long aspired to a degree of independence or dominion status within the British Empire.

In name Burma remained a crown colony, like the Straits Settlements and Hongkong, but in fact the Burmese were granted a very large measure of administrative responsibility. The British governor, appointed by the Crown, was given unusually great reserve powers, including authority in all matters pertaining to military and foreign affairs and the currency, and it was provided that in case of any emergency he could assume sweeping additional authority. The Burmese, however, elected their own parliament, with a senate and a lower house and a cabinet responsible to a premier. The governor retained supervisory power over these organizations. The vote was granted to all adult British subjects with certain not unreasonable property qualifications. This permitted the Indians to vote— a measure which occasioned great ill will on the part of the Burmese, as did repeated interferences on the part of the governor in matters which the natives wished to manage in their own way and to their own advantage.

Burma was split into seven divisions, and each division was administered by a commissioner appointed by the governor. The divisions, in turn, were split into many districts, in each of which a deputy commissioner held the power of last appeal. Every village elected its own headman, who acted as interpreter of the orders of the Government and, moreover, collected village taxes.

On paper the plan looked sound and seemed generous. But it failed to work smoothly. The Burmese thought they were capable of a wider latitude of administration of their own affairs and resented what they called "British meddling." The British were convinced that, because of native lack of education and training in government, supervision could not be further relaxed. This situation led to conflicts, repressive measures, sullen resentment. When the Japanese invaders arrived this unhappy state of affairs resulted in widespread native sabotage of British defense and supply measures and in fifth-column activities which were of enormous assistance to the enemy.

Industrialization had not made much progress in Burma. There were refineries to handle the growing production of the Burmese oil fields. There were rice mills, and there were sawmills to handle the immense export of teak from the forested mountains high up the great rivers draining into the Irrawaddy.

In addition to the vast strategic value of Burma, the capture of which cut off China from land routes for the importation of essential war supplies and created a threat to India, particularly to Bengal, which is highly anti-British, the value of Burma as a source of food supply is enormous to the Japanese Army. Before the invasion Burma was sending an average of 2,000,000 tons of rice to India every year and an additional 375,000 tons to Ceylon. Not only is this rice supply of vital importance to Japan, but the loss of it complicates the British problem of feeding India and Ceylon.

In addition to the rice, Japan is now obtaining tungsten, nickel, lead, cotton, oil, and timber from Burma. Zinc and copper were also mined, and the country was producing nearly 1,300 ounces of gold and more than 5,500,000 ounces of silver annually.

In 1939 Burma's mines produced 59,000 long tons of zinc, which is probably ample for all Japan's needs. The last year for which statistics are known showed that Japan imported only 48,000 tons of zinc. For some unknown reason the great Baldwin mines, smelters, and refineries near Lashio were not destroyed when the British evacuated. In 1939 the Namtu smelters in the Lashio district produced more than

77,000 metric tons of lead. Japan's annual consumption of
lead in 1939 totaled 120,000 tons, so the Burma output will
satisfy more than half her requirements measured on consumption before she plunged into all-out war. Burma's
tungsten production in 1939 exceeded 6,500 metric tons,
and this, too, now goes to the enemy.

In contrast to Burma's zinc, lead, and tungsten mines and
handling plants, which were left intact, Burma's oil wells
were subjected to the "scorched-earth" policy, but it is
expected that the Japanese will have brought the fields into
full production again early in 1943. These oil fields yielded
335,000,000 gallons of high-grade oil in 1940.

Control of Burma is of supreme importance to Japan.
Not only does this control cut off China from all except
aerial connection with her allies, but it protects Japan's
positions in Malaya, Thailand, and Indo-China. In addition
it makes the Bay of Bengal of little value to the United
Nations, for not only does Burma afford Japan air fields
within five hundred miles of India, but her hold upon the
Andaman Islands places all shipping en route to Calcutta
at the mercy of her bombing planes. As a result the supply-
ing of India and China with war material must now be
carried on largely through the port of Bombay, far away
on India's western coast.

India's most important industrial districts, when war supplies and manufactures are considered, are the Bengal,
Orissa, and Bihar coal- and iron-mining areas, and these

are now within easy bombing range of Japanese-held bases
in Burma. When the Japanese bombed Rangoon and other
Burmese centers, 90 per cent of the Burmese workmen fled.
If bombings in India have the same result, the industrial
areas of eastern India may be made useless to the United
Nations, even if the bombers do not actually destroy the
plants which have been turning out an ever-increasing flow
of war supplies.

The mountain barriers between Burma and India were
considered so impenetrable that the only British reinforce-
ments sent from India to aid the outnumbered defenders of
Burma consisted of a single battalion of troops ferried there
by airplane. But subsequently, after the debacle, tens of
thousands of Burmese, Indians, and British managed to
reach safety in India by following the trails through from
one hundred to three hundred miles of jungle-covered
mountains, and some of the harassed troops got out that
way too. This great trek of refugees proved to the dismayed
United Nations staffs in India that the mountain passes
could be utilized by a Japanese army bent upon invading
India. The Japanese accomplishment of the "impossible"
conquest of Malaya by the mainland jungle route has
shown that India is not so safe on the Burmese flank as she
was once thought to be.

The material and political rehabilitation of Burma will be
a titanic task. The destruction wrought by the Japanese
invasion will require an enormous quantity of money and

of work, and this destruction will probably be doubled during the campaign which will be necessary to drive out the conquerors. Burma, like Korea and other distinctly nationalistic countries on the eastern Asiatic mainland, will have to undergo a period of political tutelage and education and carefully planned economic rehabilitation. The Burmese will not want this to be carried on under exclusively British direction. Here, again, is a job which seemingly can be accomplished only by some international authority or agency. China will be vitally interested in the future of Burma; because she needs access to the Indian Ocean by way of Burma she should certainly be well represented on any commission or organization which will have the task of bringing order out of chaos there. And the United States, as the most powerful of the sponsors of the Atlantic Charter, will be expected to shoulder much of the work and responsibility—and the burden of financing, too.

Burma is another area of the Far East that will look to us to be at the least a firm umpire and adjudicator after the war. More millions of dark-skinned, dark-eyed people, holding us under a hopeful and speculative gaze! We cannot face them if we fail them. It is no longer a question as to whether we have the hardihood to take up the labor that lies ahead. The question is whether we have the hardihood and narrow selfishness to refuse and to try to shirk our destiny in Asia.

CHAPTER XIII

And India

IN SPITE OF THE MANNER in which the whole issue of India has been obscured in the United States by millions of words about Gandhi's idealism and mysticism, the one fact that really stands out crystal-clear in his conduct during the war is that he is a tough-minded realist and an immensely clever politician. Stripped of his "atmospheric accessories," such as his loincloth, his frugality, his goat's milk, and his spinning wheel, Gandhi emerges as a political leader who believes that the Axis will win the war. He has played his political game so that if the Axis Powers win he will be able to ask favors of them, even to demand India's independence as a reward for what he has done to embarrass and frustrate the war efforts of the United Nations.

His is a game which cannot be lost, for Britain is already pledged to give India freedom virtually on her own terms as soon after hostilities cease as the Indian groups can frame their own constitution. If the chances of an Axis victory are conceded to be 50 per cent, or even lower than that, Gandhi can still feel that he is taking a chance which any shrewd gambler would approve. The All-India Congress is now in a position to demand the promised freedom if the United Nations win; if the United Nations lose, Gandhi and his adherents can say to the Axis: "We have not helped the British and Americans and Chinese—we have hindered them. Give us our reward."

The justice of this summary of Gandhi's policies and position becomes clear if his record is examined in relation to Japan's timetable of conquest. Even just after Dunkirk, and during the summer when Britain was suffering the blitzkrieg, Gandhi solemnly stated: "We do not seek our independence out of Britain's ruin. That is not the way of non-violence." And Nehru, on May 20, 1940, declared: "Launching a civil-disobedience campaign at a time when Britain is engaged in a life-and-death struggle would be an act derogatory to India's honor." As late as November 1941, less than a month before Japan attacked Pearl Harbor, Gandhi publicly declared that a mass movement during the war would be "unthinkable," that it would merely be taking advantage of Britain's difficulties and would lead to violence and civil war.

Then came Japan's victorious march southward. Colonial Britain was proved to be almost powerless even in self-defense. Hongkong, Malaya, Singapore, Rangoon, and Burma fell to the Japanese in rapid succession. Malaya and Burma taught the bitter lesson that political weakness can outweigh armies and armament. Munitions alone do not bring victory, and a successful defensive is almost impossible in a country where the natives not only give no fighting support but even organize hostile guerrillas.

Lord Beaverbrook, in a broadcast to Canada on March 2, 1942, said: "Singapore was not lost because of superior equipment. On the contrary, the weight of munitions was on our side."

The events of the Japanese southward campaigns, admissions like those of Beaverbrook, and known facts concerning the collapses in Malaya and in Burma gave Gandhi his cue.

Actually India is not a Pacific country and does not come in the geographical area which is the main subject of treatment in this book. But because India adjoins Burma and China, both subjected to Japanese attack, and because the sincerity of the professions of the United Nations may be judged by Britain's acts in India and by American vocal or silent approval of those acts, India cannot be divorced from the problems of East Asia. Certainly geographically and in view of Japan's sustained propaganda campaign concerning "Asia for the Asiatics," India falls more naturally into the Pacific area of conflict than into the European-Soviet zone.

Japan's assault on the democracies means the end of imperialism in India just as much as it does in China or in Hongkong, and India will necessarily have to share the benefits and disabilities accruing to the rest of Asia as a result of this war.

The future of India has become the concern of the United States. Already global strategy has placed American troops beside Indian troops fighting in the desert west of Egypt, and American troops and fliers are stationed in India ready to help repel any Japanese attempt at invasion. American fliers based upon India not only ferry war supplies to China but use Indian bases for raids on the Japanese in Burma and for bombing forays against Japanese transports and naval ships in the Bay of Bengal.

Washington has been chary of making open suggestions to London about how to handle the Indian problem. Indeed, the problem itself changes from week to week, and it will continue to change with dismaying rapidity. It is primarily Britain's problem—and India's. But if India should openly join the United Nations, then the United States would be jointly responsible for India's ultimate independence. We are already committed to assuring her *ultimate* independence, because of our glittering promises to all peoples that they shall have the four freedoms. But until we have helped to win the war we shall probably not meddle in the British-India dispute unless both sides first let us know secretly that our mediation would be welcome.

The history of the All-India National Congress party for the last decade furnishes many contradictions. The party officially went on record as protesting against the Japanese invasion of Manchuria, the Italian invasion of Ethiopia, and the fascist meddling in Spain. Sympathy was shown for China by large cash collections from the public and heavy shipments of drugs and surgical supplies. Japanese goods were boycotted as a result of Japan's invasion of China, and the party denounced appeasement policies in Europe long before the Chamberlain Government in Britain fell into wide disrepute.

The Congress party has also experienced dramatic changes in strength. After a rapid growth, membership fell to half a million following the failure of the civil-disobedience campaign in 1934. Then came a resurgence, and by 1937 membership totaled 3,000,000, and in 1939 it reached more than 5,000,000.

In many quarters the Congress party is lightly dismissed because of a mistaken belief that it represents only Hindus and is therefore non-representative of the people of India as a whole. Actually, however, the party is vigorous and powerful and has commanded widespread support. Membership in the party includes not only Hindus but also Sikhs, Moslems, untouchables, Brahmans, landlords and peasants, illiterates and scholars, merchants and union workers, and subjects of the native princes and of British India as well.

It is this diversification of allegiances which makes the problem of India so difficult of solution. Mohammed Ali Jinnah, president of the All-India Moslem League, declared publicly after the arrests of Gandhi and Nehru late in the summer of 1942 that if Britain acceded to the Congress demands "Moslem India would regard it as a gross betrayal of Moslem rights and a breach of faith with Moslem India." A holy war against Britain in India would set all the Near East aflame.

If British policy results in rebellion by Congress supporters, India will be open to Japanese invasion. If British policy pacifies the Congress adherents, then the Moslems might take action which would result in Egypt, Turkey, and many other vitally important areas being easily overrun by the European members of the Axis group.

Actually Jinnah and the Moslem League no more represent all the 90,000,000 Moslems in India than the Congress party represents all the Hindus. In 1937, when elections were being held for the legislatures in the eleven provinces, 480 seats were reserved for the Moslem League, but they won only 114. Out of an estimated 7,300,000 Moslem votes only 321,000 were cast for League candidates, which is 4.6 per cent of the total. Neither in Sind nor in the Northwest Frontier Province, both of which have Moslem majorities of population, was a single League representative elected. The League is openly in favor of *Pakistan*, or the partitioning of India between Moslems and Hindus, but the

Shiah sect, comprising one fifth of all Moslems, opposes *Pakistan* and supports the Congress party, as does the numerically strong Moslem sect called the Jamiat-ul-Ulema.

Britain also has definite treaty obligations to the 563 native states and their princes, and the combined populations of these semi-autonomous areas within India itself total more than 80,000,000, amongst whom there is no unity of policy or desire in such matters as self-rule or independence or allegiance to any Indian political party.

Regardless of prejudices or sympathies which different Americans may have concerning the continuing political crisis in India, it cannot be denied with any justification or showing of fairness that England has done the most magnificent job of administration in India that the world has ever seen conferred on any subject people. Our own record in the Philippines was excellent, but we had there only a population of a little more than 7,000,000 to begin with, and 16,000,000 when the Japanese drove us out. In area, too, the comparison is grotesque. India covers 1,819,000 square miles, the Philippines only 114,400.

In India the population increases at the rate of nearly 5,000,000 a year. British statistics say that between 1931 and 1941 the population rose by nearly 50,000,000 and stood at 388,000,000 when the last census was taken. Fully 95 per cent of these millions are villagers and peasants, and yet in spite of tremendous efforts with irrigation and drainage projects the British were able to increase the area

of tillable land only from 229,000,000 acres in 1931 to
231,000,000 acres by 1937, after which the outbreak of war
in Europe curtailed this type of development.

The so-called "brutal oppression" of India was carried on
by 65,000 British civilians and a British army which, before
the war, never exceeded 50,000 men. The central, provincial, and local governments employ upward of 1,500,000
persons, and there were more than 1,000,000 men in the
Indian Army before Japan brought the war to the Pacific
in 1941. All of them were volunteers. The civilian government employees and armed Indians, then, together totaled
more than 2,500,000 men, and the British of all classes
115,000. These figures alone reveal the stupidity of many
charges made against the British by a certain type of rabble
rouser who for obscure reasons likes to foment unjustified
criticism and misunderstanding of all things British all over
the world.

Sir Stafford Cripps, who took compromise proposals to
India in the spring of 1942, charged in July that Gandhi,
unprepared to wait for promised freedom after the war,
"would rather jeopardize the freedom and the whole cause
of the United Nations." British, American, Chinese, and
Indian soldiers are engaged in this conflict, Sir Stafford
declared, and "cannot be sacrificed in the gallant struggle
for the liberty of the world by a political party maneu-
vering in India or in any other country."

In a broadcast directed to the United States, Cripps

charged that Gandhi "threatens extremes of pressure in this most difficult hour to win political power for his party. He may gain a measure of support for his mass disobedience but, for the sake of India as well as for the cause of the United Nations, it will be our duty to insist on keeping India as a safe and orderly base for our operations against the Japanese. . . . We cannot allow the actions of a visionary, however distinguished in the fight for freedom in the past, to thwart the United Nations in their drive for victory in the East."

The arrest of Gandhi and other Congress party leaders was neither ordered, proposed, nor initiated from London. It was a measure ordered by the Central Government of India, and this consists of the Viceroy and a Council of fifteen members, of whom only four are British and eleven are Indians, representing many religions and districts and varying shades of political thought. True, London could have revoked the order for the arrests, but New Delhi made the decision.

The four British on the Council are Sir Archibald Wavell, War Member; Sir Reginald Maxwell, Home Department; Sir Edward Benthall, War Transport; and Sir Jeremy Raisman, Finance.

The eleven Indians on the Council, and their portfolios, are as follows: Sir J. P. Srivastava, Member for Civil Defense; N. R. Sarker, Member for Commerce; M. A. Aney, Member for Indians Overseas; Sir H. P. Mody, Member for

Supply; Dr. B. R. Ambedkar, Member for Labour; Sir C. P. Ramaswami, Information Member; Sir Jogendra Singh, Member of Education, Lands, and Health; Sir Mahomed Usman, Member for Posts and Air; Sir Firozkhan Noon, Member for Defense; Sir Syed Sultan Ahmed, Law Member; and Sir A. Ramaswami Mudaliar is Member without Portfolio.

It is true that final veto power and extraordinary powers to meet any emergency rest with the Viceroy and the British Cabinet, but these powers have been rarely exercised for the last twenty years. In fiscal affairs India has had full control of her tariffs, taxation, and trade, and there has been no intervention from the Viceroy or from London since 1921. Britain has, however, reserved the power to say the final word in all matters relating to defense and military operations, and on all policies which might occasion domestic conflicts in India itself between Hindus and Moslems or other elements of the population.

The Congress party's rejection of the Cripps offer was based on the position that a free and democratic India would associate herself with other free nations in the war against aggression—but it demanded complete control of the defense measures. This, Cripps said, was a transfer of responsibility impossible to contemplate in wartime.

The Congress reply was that only a free India could be galvanized into resistance against invasion—in other words, "Give us our freedom now, or we not only shall not help you to repel the Japanese, but we shall do all we can by strikes, non-payment of taxes, interference with transportation, and the like to hamstring your own efforts against your enemy. We shall not hold Japan our enemy unless you first give us freedom and the right to handle our own defense."

This is high-sounding argument, in the original All-India Congress phrasing, and it confuses and deceives many people, particularly in this country. Actually it is politics playing a selfish and opportunist game with stakes belonging to other people who are fighting for their lives. Gandhi and the All-India Congress party are not concerned lest China's last air supply line be entirely cut off by a Japanese invasion or lest the United Nations be subjected to a defeat in a vital area of the war.

It is true that an India ruled by force and subdued by bamboo beatings and shootings seems to be an India already mortgaged to the enemy. It is also true, unhappily, that a repressive policy in India is likely to cost the United Nations, as a group, the faith and confidence of millions of the peoples of Asia. But the United Nations, like the All-India Congress party, are being forced to gamble for high stakes. India is a huge reservoir of raw and manufactured material and of potential man power. It must be made into a base as strong as Australia for an eventual counteroffensive against Japan. It must be held in order that China may not be entirely cut off from outside aid except by way of

Russia. The Japanese must be kept out, not only lest they make the Persian Gulf unsafe for United Nations shipping, but lest from India they make a junction with Axis armies if the Germans break through the Middle East.

It is certain that India cannot be properly held without the good will of the people, and how this good will can be earned and held without antagonizing powerful minorities is an age-old problem in that great subcontinent. At present most Indians see no incentive to fighting and dying in order to perpetuate the existing rule, and they so hate the existing rule that they have no active desire to co-operate in defense just because of a promise of freedom after the war has ended.

The hatreds of today and the mistakes of the past cannot permanently obscure the fact that Britain has brought to India a long peace, has nurtured the idea of unity, has conferred enormous physical and educational benefits, has introduced modern transportation, has nearly abolished famine, and has fought a slowly winning battle against caste, suttee, and purdah. The tendency amongst the people of India and amongst millions of other Asians, however, is to forget these things and to hear only the whip of the lash or the crack of the revolver used today to suppress today's lawlessness.

It is astonishing that so large a proportion of public opinion in the United States sympathizes with Gandhi and his followers and disregards the larger issues at stake. After all, we laud the courage and loyalty of the Filipinos for fighting with us from Lingayen Gulf to Bataan and on Corregidor. The Filipinos had been promised independence in 1946. The people of India have been promised independence immediately after the war. The Filipinos did not try to sabotage our defense efforts in their islands by declaring that they would not fight unless we gave them independence immediately. Had they done so, American rage at such a betrayal would have been white-hot. Why, then, does so much of the American public condone precisely such an obstructionist attitude on the part of the clique which Gandhi controls in India?

CHAPTER XIV

What of Australia?

SINCE OCTOBER 7, 1941, when the Curtin Government attained power at Canberra with a membership made up exclusively of Labour party personnel, Australia has been making history in the Pacific and in the British Empire at a rate little understood in the United States.

The great continental Commonwealth has created for itself, in spite of opposition from London and from its own Conservatives, a new alignment with the United States which may have effects of astounding importance by the end of the war. In addition to this, Australia has ventured independently into world diplomacy, has framed its own policy toward Soviet Russia, and has developed an entirely new and startling relationship toward Great Britain and the rest of the Empire. And, in spite of London's cautious policy toward India, Australia has openly expressed sympathy for the subject peoples of Asia.

For these achievements credit must be given primarily to two men, John Curtin, the Prime Minister, and Dr. Herbert Vere Evatt, Minister of External Affairs and Attorney General. The Labour party's unique foreign policies began to develop obscurely as recently as 1936, but attained maturity with great rapidity under Curtin and Evatt after the attack on Pearl Harbor, and particularly during the days when the weakness of Singapore became apparent.

It is curious that the American press has not made these developments clear to the public in the United States but has, instead, devoted most of its Australian news and comments to the presence of General Douglas MacArthur and the American Expeditionary Forces there, or to essentially trivial affairs like air raids over Darwin, Port Moresby, and the Island of Timor.

During the first nine months of the war Australia emerged almost unnoticed into full and vigorous nationhood and openly courted closer relationships with the United States at the expense of relationships with London, in spite of London's opposition to these developments. There was also secret and outspoken opposition to these new policies in Canberra, Sydney, and Melbourne, particularly from the imperial-minded leaders of the Australian Conservative party.

Premier Curtin, in a declaration made only nineteen days after the attack on Pearl Harbor, used language hitherto undreamed of from any British Dominion source when he made "demands" upon both Churchill and President Roosevelt and declared that Australia refused "to accept the dictum that the Pacific struggle is a subordinate segment of the general conflict." Instead, he declared, Australia regarded the global conflict as an indivisible struggle, and he demanded for Australia a voice in general strategic planning for the Pacific area.

Curtin, one-time labor-union official and later the editor of a labor-union journal, has been titular leader of the Australian Labour party since 1935. Evatt seemed securely placed for life as one of the judges on the Commonwealth High Court, but his apprehensions about Australia's future led him in 1940 to the unprecedented step of resigning from the High Court in order to enter active politics and stand for a seat in Parliament as a Labour candidate. The obscure editor and the little-known judge seem to have been the men of the hour and have not hesitated to make international history in a manner which has won the approval of an overwhelming majority of their constituents.

The Conservative party, when R. G. Menzies was Premier and during the two-month period of office of his Conservative successor, A. W. Faddon, based its foreign and preparedness policies on implicit faith in the might of the British Navy and the supposed impregnability of Singapore. The only evidence the Conservatives gave of reading aright the signs of growing peril in the Pacific were the creation of legations in Washington and Tokyo in 1940 and in China in 1941. Under Menzies, Australia seemed content to play merely a minor part in the general Empire scheme of defense, although when he named a minister to Chungking he declared that this action meant that Australia regarded herself as "a principal" in the Pacific.

Two years before the outbreak of war in Europe in 1939, Curtin and his party leaders began to express fears that in case of a new Anglo-German conflict the Empire would concentrate most of its military and naval effort on defending the British Isles, the Mediterranean-Suez route, the Middle East, and India. Prior to this stirring of premonition Australia seemingly cared less about virtual Dominion autonomy than did Canada and South Africa. In fact, the Australian Parliament did not even ratify the Statute of Westminster, passed by the British Parliament as long ago as 1932.

Curtin's first serious brush with the Conservative Government was when he, as leader of the Opposition, boldly attacked the Commonwealth's reliance on British sea power when a bill was brought in providing for enlargement of the Australian Navy. A small Australian Navy would be useless without Britain's help, he pointed out, and then stressed the vital importance of air power, asking what would happen to Australia if she were to be attacked while

Britain was defensively placed during a war in Europe. Singapore, he charged, would become useless without battleships plus a vast air armada.

In November of 1936, during a debate in Parliament, Curtin asked this embarrassing question: "Would the British Government dare to authorize the dispatch of any substantial part of the fleet to the East to help Australia? Our dependence upon the competence, let alone the readiness, of British statesmen to send forces to our aid is too dangerous a hazard upon which to found Australia's defense policy."

The Conservative Government not only had agreed with London's policy of concentrating British forces and American lend-lease material in the Mediterranean area, but had committed Australia to adhering to the general imperial defense policy. Australian troops were sent wherever consultants in London decided that they were most needed. One result of this was loss on a vast scale of men and munitions, guns and planes in Greece and Crete. Had part of what was lost in those ill-advised ventures been sent to Malaya, Japan's southward advance might have been checked, saving Australia from the danger of invasion.

Eventually Australia lost more than 12,000 men killed and captured in the African campaigns and another 18,000 killed or captured in Malaya and at the fall of Singapore. There was a large body of Australian troops in North Africa when the Japanese attacked in the Pacific. It was privately announced that they were going back to Australia to defend their homeland, whether the British high command liked the move or not. The British had to pretend to like it, and these forces reached Australia late in March.

When the Curtin Government took office in October 1941, exactly two months before Japan attacked Pearl Harbor, general military and diplomatic policies, framed on the assumption of the inevitability of war in the Pacific, were adopted at secret sessions of the Cabinet, but these general decisions were only revealed piecemeal later in different addresses made to Parliament by the Prime Minister and the Minister of External Affairs.

First, it was decided not to try to back out of any commitments previously made in the interests of imperial defense, but in future to concentrate new efforts on Australia's home defense and to help bolster the forces in Malaya and at Singapore. This decision was linked to a formal but secret request that Britain strengthen Singapore and grant to Australia a full partner's share in all decisions regarding that great naval base. One result of this was the dispatch of the ill-fated *Repulse* and *Prince of Wales* to Malayan waters. At that time Australia made no move to decrease her forces in North Africa or to curtail the shipment of Australian-made planes and guns promised to various British fronts.

Late in November, Dr. Evatt told Parliament that Canberra had made it plain to London that Australia would never ratify any appeasement move or any agreement which Great Britain might make with Japan that would be detrimental to China. He also announced a notification to London that Australia believed that, where negotiations with Japan were concerned, "the leadership and the initiative should be retained by the United States on behalf of the democratic powers." Dr. Evatt also disclosed at this time that a cardinal principle of Australian diplomacy favored an alliance with Soviet Russia and "a firm and unbroken alliance" between all the countries of the British Empire, the United States, and Russia.

Most revolutionary of all moves made by Australia at this time, however, was the secret notification sent to Great Britain that henceforth Australia would feel herself entitled to "a footing of absolute equality with the United Kingdom" in any diplomatic mission or war council organized to handle political affairs dealing with any part of the Pacific area.

When the final history of this war is written it may well be verified by documents now secret that it was Australian pressure which had much to do with Churchill's declaration to the effect that, if the United States should become involved in war with Japan, "a British declaration will follow within the hour."

Dr. Evatt has since revealed that when Japan's special emissary, Saburo Kurusu, made his November 20 proposal offering to withdraw Japan's armies from French Indo-

China, but reserving complete freedom of action regarding military moves against China or Soviet Russia, Australia objected firmly. Canberra would countenance no compromise and charged that it would be iniquitous to discountenance Japanese aggression southward but to agree tacitly to new aggressions in China or in Siberia. At this juncture, too, Australia made secret proposals for an agreement between Britain and Soviet Russia providing that if Japan should attack either power the other would automatically be bound to launch hostilities against the aggressor. It has not yet been explained why this proposal failed of adoption or whether it was refused by Moscow or London or both.

It was on Monday, December 8, that Australia made both international and British Empire history. On that day the Commonwealth declared war against Japan, Finland, Hungary, and Rumania. And then, for the first time in Empire history, and solely to emphasize its autonomous status, Australia arranged to have the war declarations submitted directly to King George without having any of the British Cabinet ministers participate in the ceremony in any way. This was done, it was later explained to Parliament at Canberra, "to express clearly the unbroken line of prerogative authority, and at the same time to make it clear that The King was acting exclusively on the advice of his Ministers in the Commonwealth." The United Kingdom had nothing to do with the event except to marvel and to surmise.

On September 3, 1939, when the Conservative party was in power, it had merely announced that Australia automatically found herself at war with Germany because Britain had declared the existence of a state of hostilities.

Premier Churchill was in the United States at Christmastime in 1941, and on December 26 he addressed a joint session of the American Congress. He candidly admitted the gloomy prospect of being forced to adhere to defensive strategy all during 1942 and said that the offensive might possibly be taken on a grand scale in 1943. He admitted that the Pacific area of conflict had suffered and would continue to suffer because of the necessity for bending all energies and utilizing all resources for the struggles around the British Isles, in Libya, and "in the battle of the Atlantic upon which all depends."

Prime Minister Curtin then telephoned twice to the White House and talked to both Churchill and President Roosevelt. Then, on December 27, he made a sensational public statement in which he declared:

We refuse to accept the dictum that the Pacific struggle is a subordinate segment of the general conflict. The Australian Government therefore regards the Pacific struggle as primarily one in which the United States and Australia must have the fullest say in the direction of the fighting plan. Australia looks to America free of any pangs as to our traditional links of kinship with the United Kingdom. We know that Australia can go and Britain can still hold on. Australian policy will be shaped towards obtaining Russian aid and working out with the United States as the major factor a plan of Pacific strategy along with the British, Chinese and Dutch forces.

After Churchill's return to England there began the long struggle over the feasibility of an Imperial War Cabinet in London and a Pacific War Council there too. Australia and New Zealand wanted the Pacific War Council located in Washington. Late in January, Churchill told the Commons that Canada and South Africa did not care to have representatives in an Imperial War Cabinet and that therefore he had offered all the Dominions the right to send representatives to the British War Cabinet. They were to be heard in argument and appeal, but were to have no voting power. Australia reluctantly accepted the War Cabinet arrangement and the compromise of establishing a Pacific War Council in London on which Britain, Australia, the Netherlands, and New Zealand were represented.

Late in February, Dr. Evatt made a report to Parliament at Canberra in which he stated: "We desired, above all, that the Commonwealth should have the opportunity of conferring as an ally with the United States and China at the same council table and on a common footing."

Singapore surrendered on February 15, and on that date the Curtin Government made secret proposals that General MacArthur be smuggled away from the Philippines and be given supreme command in the Pacific southwest with headquarters in Australia, which was proposed as the springboard for a vigorous counterattack against Japan. Washington agreed at once, but it was not until February 22 that British acceptance of the plan was signified. The public was not informed until March 17, when MacArthur arrived in Australia.

Meanwhile Java and Rangoon had fallen on the same day, March 10, and London's prime concern was the safety of India and the Middle East.

The day after the secret agreement to shift General MacArthur to Australia, President Roosevelt broadcast a fireside chat to the nation in which he said, in part:

For forty years it has always been our strategy that in the event of a full-scale attack on the [Philippine] Islands by Japan we should fight a delaying action. . . . We knew that the war as a whole would have to be fought and won by a process of attrition against Japan itself. We knew all along that with our greater resources we could outbuild Japan and ultimately overwhelm her. . . . We knew that to obtain our objective many varieties of operations would be necessary in areas other than the Philippines. Nothing that has occurred in the past two months has caused us to revise this basic strategy.

Australia was gratified at the President's acknowledgment that the Far Pacific was one of the vitally important war areas, but was gloomy over his reference to the necessity for proceeding slowly against the Japanese and at his hints of a prolonged period of defensive strategy.

It is a curious fact that many newspapers in the United States did not print the more somber portions of the President's fireside chat. One result of this was the quick spread of unjustified optimism in this country and eager hopes for an almost immediate general offensive.

With General MacArthur's arrival in Australia, the Commonwealth immediately renewed complaints against the inadequacy of the Pacific War Council in London, even though membership had been widened by the admittance of the Chinese ambassador there, Dr. Wellington Koo. The Australians complained, and with complete justice, that when they wished to contact Washington on matters of immediate importance they had to work through half a dozen intermediaries. A matter must first be referred to the Australian War Cabinet, then to the Imperial War Cabinet in London, then to the Pacific War Council in London, then to the combined United Nations chiefs of staff in London. From London the matter would be referred to President Roosevelt, and he in turn would refer it to the chiefs of staff in Washington. This cumbersome and absurd arrangement, Prime Minister Curtin insisted, could be ended only by the establishment of a genuine Pacific War Council in Washington.

A week before MacArthur reached Australia, Premier Curtin made a broadcast to the United States in which he announced that he was sending Dr. Evatt to this country to "seek the counsel and advice of President Roosevelt." This move shocked London seriously, even though Curtin softened the announcement by paying tribute to Britain for having won the long battle in the air in 1940 and adding that Australia realized that Great Britain had a paramount obligation to supply Russia, "and she cannot at the same time go all out in the Pacific." Dr. Evatt reached Washington on March 20, and just ten days later President Roosevelt announced that a Pacific War Council had been set up there, including the United States, Australia, China, New Zealand, Canada, Britain, and the Netherlands.

Australia had finally maneuvered herself (and New Zealand) into general staff and policy discussions and decisions on a footing of equality with the United States and Great Britain. This meant that she had achieved full partnership, as a nation, in the conduct of the war.

Australia realizes that her great continent now stands in the same danger of invasion in which England stood after Dunkirk, with the important difference that England then stood alone, while Australia has the American Army, Navy, and Air Force to look to for ever-increasing help. Nevertheless, invasion may materialize at any time.

But in spite of this peril the Australian Government and people are demanding the early establishment of a "second front" in their part of the globe. They want Australian troops in the vanguard of the forces that must push Japan back into her own islands. They realize that overwhelming air power alone can accomplish this difficult feat, and that the islands of the East Indies and the Philippines must be regarded, strategically, as merely "unsinkable aircraft carriers." By using those islands in place of aircraft carriers, the Australians believe, an offensive can be waged successfully without enduring the wearying processes of awaiting battleship, cruiser, and destroyer construction.

Australia's postwar future is difficult to guess about at present. The Commonwealth has only about 7,500,000 inhabitants, and an area almost precisely equal to that of continental United States, not including Alaska. The tropical portion of Australia and the great inland deserts will never support a large population, but it is estimated that the more temperate part of the continent could support about 25,000,000 people at the white man's standard of well-being.

Australia has deliberately limited immigration, even of whites, and is still ready to fight to maintain her "white Australia" policy. Immigration restrictions, coupled with individual and corporate ownership of vast tracts of idle lands, have combined to retard population growth.

Although more than 95 per cent of the inhabitants are of the stock of the British Isles, the Commonwealth seems to have less sentimental attachment to Britain than any of the other Dominions, and the calamities of Greece, Crete, Malaya, and Singapore have combined to create a harshly critical attitude toward the mother country.

Before we became allies against the Axis Powers, Australia's liking and admiration for the United States was deep and genuine, and there was a noticeable tendency toward closer cultural, economic, and co-operative relations with this country. Unhappily the presence of a large American Expeditionary Force in Australia can easily blight this cordiality of feeling. A couple of military rape cases will more than offset the work of half a dozen goodwill missions. And the Australians are a sensitive and justly proud people. It will require extreme tact on the part of all of our higher command to avoid unintentionally antagonizing large elements of the Australian public.

The war, and especially ultimate success, may strengthen the "go it alone" sentiment which is already noticeable in the Commonwealth. But an Australia with only 7,500,000 people cannot assure its own safety, much less take a leading part in underwriting the future stability of the Far Pacific.

Already there is a powerful movement in Australia to waken the whole people to the inevitable obligations of the peace. Even the Government is preaching that Australia, after the winning of the war, must not merely try to make itself snug and comfortable and then evade its international duties. A broadcast officially sponsored in midsummer of 1942 warned:

Shrill voices will be raised, demanding that our Government's sole duty will be to protect our living standards, our comforts, our investments, and that the mortal sickness of humanity abroad is none of our affair. . . . It is enough to say that if we and other nations refuse to see that neither peace, nor better living standards, nor any other things we hope for in a better world can be won by purely national effort, but are possible only by intense international cooperation, all the disasters of the last ten years will surely be upon us again.

Australia has been fighting for the cause of democracy magnificently for more than three years. Her sacrifices and contributions have been out of proportion to her man power and her wealth. She has certainly earned the right to decide her own destiny when the United Nations finally win this war.

CHAPTER XV

New Zealand Looks Ahead

ALTHOUGH a United Nations victory will unquestionably bring about profound changes in the status of India and may see a drastic alteration of the relationship of Australia to the British Empire, New Zealand not only will not seek any different status than that which she now enjoys, but will even probably stoutly resist any loosening of the imperial ties.

New Zealand is as English as Sussex or Surrey, and at the same time as Scotch as the Highlands. Even military disasters as destructive to New Zealand troops as the fall of Singapore was to the magnificent Australian contingent there will not provoke New Zealanders into critical antagonism to the British scheme of things.

New Zealand has been prosperous and contented under a system whereby she sold more than 75 per cent of all her products to Great Britain and relied for her safety on the British Navy. The fact that today it is the American Navy and Air Force that have so far kept the Dominion safe from Japanese attack makes no difference to the New Zealander. He is confident that at the end of the war things will return to "the good old ways." In fact, his conservatism in matters of empire is in startling contrast to his radicalism in social and economic legislation and experiment.

The only changes the New Zealanders desire are those designed to "make the Dominion a better place, socially and economically, for the boys in the armed services to return to after the war is over." And this will be a large order, for already the man power of the country is so seriously depleted, and already taxes are so high, that there seems to be little margin of productive possibility or increasing wealth with which to finance additional projects for public welfare.

With a population of 1,600,000, New Zealand has an estimated 350,000 males of military age, but after three years of war the little country has mobilized more than half its male population, or upward of 400,000 men, for one or another branch of the armed forces, has lost nearly 15,000 soldiers killed, wounded, missing, or prisoners of war, and has called into uniform every able-bodied male between the ages of twenty and sixty, irrespective of family liabilities.

It would be wrong to say that New Zealand fears a Japanese invasion; actually the country calmly expects it, and defense measures have been thorough. Plans have been perfected for evacuating the cities and shore areas likely to be attacked. Supplementary hospital accommodation is ample. All the beaches are disfigured with barbed-wire entanglements in depth, and nearly every front or back yard has its own shelter trench. In every city all parks, playgrounds, and vacant lands are scarred by deep shelter trenches.

Although New Zealand has a Labour Government, emergency war orders infringing on many of the rights for which labor has fought for years have been calmly accepted. The first such order, issued soon after Japan attacked Malaya, declared specified industries as essential and placed a legal obligation upon labor and management to sustain production. No employee in an essential industry may terminate his engagement or transfer to a new job without the consent of government man-power boards, and none can be discharged without such consent.

In the United States there has been a tremendous political and propaganda conflict over such questions as the 40-hour week, the freezing of prices and wage levels, and other measures to increase production and check inflation. But the question of the length of the labor week is one issue over which there has been no clash in New Zealand. Before the war the workers and the Labour Government zealously guarded the hard-won 40-hour five-day working week. This has been voluntarily abandoned for the duration of the war. The wages and hours agreements have been modified to provide a six-day working week of 50 hours, and only after 50 hours of labor is the time-and-a-half for overtime provision of the law applied. Former pay scales applying to the 40-hour week now apply to the 50-hour week. Overtime is limited to four hours weekly per man, which makes a 54-hour week the maximum in all industries and limits each worker to time-and-a-half pay for only four hours. There is no extra overtime pay for work on Sundays or holidays.

Price- and wage-control measures have been so successful and so well enforced that the cost of living has increased less than 10 per cent since the war began in September 1939.

With an area slightly more than twice that of the State of New York, and with a total population considerably less than that of the island of Manhattan, New Zealand nevertheless carries on magnificently as a self-governing nation. The New Zealanders number approximately as many people as are claimed by Los Angeles or Detroit. But those American cities would each have to put 400,000 men into uniform and would have to spend about $345,000,000 each on the support of the war in order to equal the New Zealand contribution to the world-wide struggle.

This small and isolated Dominion—even Australia, its nearest neighbor, is more than 1,200 miles away across the Tasman Sea—has long sustained a system of compulsory unionism under which strikes are forbidden. In all cases of labor disputes appeals to arbitration courts are compulsory, and both labor unions and employers' associations are forced to abide by the awards of these courts.

Old-age pensions, still a novelty in the United States, have been in effect in New Zealand for years. They are automatic for all women past the age of sixty and men past sixty-five and are operated entirely on a non-contributory basis. Free state-owned hospitals are also maintained for the aged who are afflicted by sickness.

The old-age pensions have been growing progressively, and the ultimate maximum pensions which will be provided by accumulating funds will, about twenty years from now, give each qualified individual an income of 30 shillings a week, or 78 pounds annually. This will mean three pounds a week for every aged couple in New Zealand, and, since payments begin automatically when the specified ages are reached, there can be no test or proof of means of subsistence required from anyone. In 1939 the old-age pensions totaled 12 pounds 10 shillings annually; in 1942 the sum was advanced to 20 pounds a year, and the progression will be gradual until the maximum of 78 pounds is attained.

The purchasing power of the New Zealand pound, in New Zealand, averages a little more than the purchasing power of $5 in American money in this country, although because of the war and pegged exchange the value of the pound of this Dominion, like that of Australia, is $3.32 in United States currency.

Widows have long been pensioned at approximately one pound a week, with an additional 10 shillings weekly for every child less than sixteen years of age.

Another highly successful New Zealand innovation is Government life and fire insurance, both written at what are said to be the lowest rates anywhere in the world. The fire insurance is profitable to the Government, but life-insurance premiums are so low that the profit margin can be but small.

New Zealand also has a free state-supported maternity service and claims the lowest mother and infant mortality rate in the world. The Maternal and Child Welfare Association, which gives both parent and infant free medical care and advice until the child is two years of age, is also free, being subsidized by the state. Free dental clinics are provided for all children from the age of five to the age of twelve years. Most of New Zealand's schools have a highly efficient free medical service, including health camps for invalid or convalescent children. This is supported by a voluntary organization, with help from the Government, and is Government-controlled.

Only 10 per cent of the hospitals in New Zealand are private institutions. In the 90 per cent which are Government-owned, care and treatment have been free since the beginning of 1940. To all families with incomes under 5 pounds a week, sickness benefits of 4 shillings weekly for every sick child less than sixteen years of age are now available. The Social Security Fund pays "illness benefits" approximating the size of old-age pensions to everyone more than sixteen years of age who is incapacitated by illness, and pays the same sums as "subsistence" to unemployed.

Partial support is extended to the 10 per cent of the hospitals which are privately owned by giving them a subsidy of slightly more than 2 pounds a week per patient. For hospitalization purposes New Zealand is divided into 42 districts. Fifty per cent of the hospital expenses are raised by local taxation and the other 50 per cent are donated by the Dominion Government, but all management is in the hands of local boards elected within the districts in which the local taxes are levied.

Late in 1941 free general medical services were made available to the public. This legislation permits the sick to choose their own doctors, but fixes the fees for daytime consultations or visits at 7 shillings 6 pence—at present exchange equal to about $1.25 in American money.

This General Medical Services statute is curious. It provides that if the patient pays the doctor, he gets a receipt for his money and is reimbursed by the State. If he cannot pay, he signs a form attesting to the treatment received, and the doctor then collects from the State. The law permits doctors to charge higher fees if they wish to do so, but the patients are not obligated to pay the overcharges, nor can the physicians collect them by going to court. Higher payment would be entirely optional and would depend on the affluence or gratitude or sense of obligation of each patient concerned.

There are certain important exclusions from the application of this General Medical Services law. The state will not pay for the treatment of venereal diseases when they are in communicable form, will not pay doctors who infringe upon dentistry by extracting teeth, will not pay for services rendered to anyone who has a claim for workers' compensation or damages, and will pay nothing if the certificate shows that sickness benefits from friendly societies or from the Social Securities sickness provision are accruing to the patient.

Consultations on Sundays, holidays, or between the hours of 9 P.M. and 7 A.M. are more profitable to the physicians, for they are paid for at the rate of 12 shillings 6 pence each. Operations, consultations between physicians, and certain specialist services do not come under this act in any way.

Parliament is now considering framing somewhat similar legislation to provide free state-paid dental care for all New Zealanders instead of merely the free dental clinics now maintained for children between the ages of five and twelve years.

The Dominion is trying to cope with the housing problem and has gone into both rental and home-building projects. More than 10,000 modern houses have been built for rental purposes. The structures are mostly frame, and those with garages command the highest rents. They are attractive. The costs of land and construction have ranged between 1,200 and 1,700 pounds each, and these homes are rented to workmen at from one pound to one pound 15 shillings per week. At present exchange levels this is equal to from $3.32 to $5.81 rent every seven days. None of these homes can be bought. The Government has figured their average life at 60 years, and under the usual amortization tables they will have yielded a profit by the end of six decades if continuously occupied.

War needs have seriously curtailed home building, but a commission is now planning a huge expansion with the coming of peace, when materials and labor will again be available.

Home owning is made easy for New Zealand workers, and would-be farmers or settlers on raw lands are also generously financed. In either case the Government will make loans up to 90 per cent of the cost of building and land, and insists only that amortization payments are so arranged that at least 60 per cent of each be repaid within a period ranging from 20 to 36 years. The interest charged on these Government loans is only $4\frac{1}{8}$ per cent a year. This system has resulted in New Zealand's having, probably, a larger percentage of privately owned homes than any other country in the world. Private loans on mortgages have been reduced to a minimum. Second mortgages are almost impossible to obtain.

New Zealand's Public Trust Office, founded as long ago as 1872, is a sore point with attorneys of the Dominion, just as the home-financing policy is a sore point with money-lenders and the Medical Services act with physicians. The Public Trust Office, conducted by the Government, administers all business affairs of prisoners and mental defectives and even probates wills at very low charges. In fact, the service is so cheap and so efficient that this Government bureau handles fully 80 per cent of all business affairs of this kind.

All these benefits have not been secured for the New Zealanders without the paying of a pretty penny by the people of the Dominion. Taxation is terrific, even before the high, practically confiscatory brackets are reached under the income-tax rates. Taxes frequently take as much as 17 ½ shillings from every pound earned—a sum equal to about 87 cents out of every dollar in American money. All unearned incomes exceeding the equivalent of $12,000 a year pay a flat rate of 90 cents in the dollar. During the first two years of New Zealand's participation in the war against Germany and Italy taxes took approximately 161 pounds from every breadwinner. Special levies take 60 per cent of wartime profits from individuals and corporations engaged in war work or war contracts—and this is on top of all other regular and emergency taxation.

New Zealand's war budget for the first two and a half years of the war totaled a little more than 104,000,000 pounds, whereas for the whole 1914–18 conflict the Dominion spent only 23,000,000 pounds on its war effort. And after this war has been won, there will be continued high taxation to finance various benefits planned for the surviving veterans. War expenditures in 1942 were estimated at three times as large as those in 1941 and were expected slightly to exceed 133,000,000 pounds.

Legislation has already been passed by Parliament to assist New Zealand soldiers who survive their service in the war. Schools and experiment stations are being prepared for those who will become farmers. After they have finished their training they may borrow from the Government up to a maximum of 3,000 pounds to purchase and build farm properties. On top of this, loans up to 1,250 pounds will be made for the purchase of livestock and farm implements. No private capital will be necessary for these men. Farm loans carry interest at 4⅛ per cent, while livestock must stagger along under 5 per cent. Ex-soldiers buying or building homes will be financed up to 100 per cent. They may borrow also up to a maximum of 1,500 pounds. Business loans will be made at the same scale and rate to discharged soldiers or sailors who can prove their aptness or ability to go into business for themselves.

These social and economic innovations might seem to show that New Zealand has no time or energy for the vigorous prosecution of her share in the war. The reverse is true. Although the Dominion already had more than

300,000 men in uniform before the Japanese attacked the democracies in the Far Pacific, the draft age has since been extended from including all males between eighteen and forty-six years of age to take in all up to fifty. Those not fitted for military service will be drafted into essential war work.

The new draft law includes women for the first time. The first class mobilized for war services included all physically fit women twenty and twenty-one years of age; and all able-bodied males remaining at home, regardless of age or occupation, are now subject to compulsory service in the Home Guard after working hours and on Sundays and on the few holidays still observed under wartime restrictions.

New Zealand's man-power contributions to the war have also been made on a gigantic scale. During the first World War, from 1914 to 1918, the Dominion forces suffered more than 60,000 killed, and the Dominion spent a total of 23,000,000 pounds on her war effort. Casualty figures for New Zealanders in the present war will be totaled on some unknown day in the far future.

New Zealand is fighting. Like her neighbor Dominion, Australia, New Zealand is the all-out ally of the United States today. Her harbors and dockyards shelter and provision and repair our naval ships and transports, her farms help to feed our American forces in Australia, and her ships and her fighting men, like those of Australia, Britain, and the Netherlands in the South Pacific area, are under the command of General Douglas MacArthur—and yet she cares for the things at home.

Fifty years ago New Zealand, because of its then advanced legislation, became known as "the laboratory of socialism." Today the people of the Dominion insist that theirs is the only country in the world where an advanced socialistic economic and governmental system has been operating with high success. They say they are determined to preserve what they have created during the last half-century, and are confident in their belief that the world of the future must be organized very much like the New Zealand of today.

But where its international political status is concerned, New Zealand wants no change and is probably the only land in the whole of the Far Pacific area that will not experience violent transitions after the United Nations win the war.

CHAPTER XVI

The Floating Fortresses

THE PACIFIC ISLANDS, other than those in the Philippine group and those of the Netherlands East Indies, which must have separate treatment, offer a difficult problem of post-war disposition. In the past most of the islands west and south of Hawaii were of little importance, but since Japan has shown the danger of such outposts in the hands of potential aggressors, and since the airplane now spans the Pacific as a matter of routine, these islands have a new value and importance. These islands, thousands of them, singly or in groups, are either owned by the United States, Britain, France, or Japan or held under mandates by the latter three powers or by Australia or New Zealand. The status of these mandates under international law would be difficult to define at present, since the mandates were supposed to be exercised under the League of Nations, and the League, if not utterly defunct, is certainly now a non-functioning body except in the case of a few minor activities and bureaus.

In the main the native populations of these islands are of the Polynesian strain, akin either to the Hawaiians or to the Maoris of New Zealand. To the southwest, Malays are numerous. Here and there are tribes still addicted to head hunting and to cannibalism. No island or group of islands has ever known any urge to nationalism or to autonomy, and government and civilization have always been imposed from outside. Roughly, these islands stretch about 5,000 miles east and west, and lie around the bulge of the globe like a gigantic belt 3,000 miles wide—1,500 miles each side of the Equator.

Commercially the islands have never been important. Most of them are of volcanic origin, though there are occasional deposits of iron ore, and France's New Caledonia produces nickel and chrome in important quantities. Exports are small in quantity and consist mostly of copra, rum, phosphates, some sugar, tapioca, coffee, bananas, vanilla, pearls, mother-of-pearl, and dried fish. Commercially they are so unimportant that they are visited only by small interisland ships, and many of the islands are without communication with the outside world for weeks and even months at a stretch.

Trading centers have grown up at a few good harbors where transpacific shipping puts in for fresh water and supplies, and there are occasional cable stations of importance. The United States has long maintained a small naval station in Samoa, and the British have a small station at Suva in the Fijis.

It remained for Japan to demonstrate the value of small Pacific islands. Going southward from Yokohama about 500 miles, the first group of what Japan has termed her "floating fortresses" is the Bonin Islands. South of these are the group of 14 islands known as the Ladrones or Marianas, which flank American Guam on the north. Flanking Guam on the south are the 549 islands of the Carolines group, and east of them are the Marshalls—60 more islands.

The Marianas, Carolines, and Marshalls have all been held by Japan under mandate from the League of Nations. They belonged to Germany before the first World War. Collectively the area is only about 950 square miles, and the total population in 1935 was given as 98,500. Under her mandate from the League, Japan was pledged not to fortify these islands, but this pledge was flouted, League inquiries were snubbed, neutral investigators were denied access to the islands, and finally Japan refused to reply to inquiries from Geneva.

From the northernmost of the Bonins to the middle of the Caroline group the north-south distance is more than 1,200 miles, and from the Carolines the chain of "floating fortresses" stretches due eastward, just north of the Equator, for more than 2,600 miles to the easternmost of the

Radak Islands in the Marshall group. Southwest of the Carolines, and east of Mindanao in the Philippines, is another cluster of Japanese-mandated islands, the Palaus or Pelews, thus extending Japan's lines another 1,200 miles in the general direction of the East Indies.

While the United States and Great Britain were living up to the treaty obligations reached at the Washington Conference in 1922, when the Nine Power Treaty was signed, and refraining from fortifying Guam, reinforcing Corregidor, or strengthening Hongkong, Japan was busy breaking her pledge about her mandated islands. Wherever good harbors occurred she built small stations to fuel and provision her Navy and to care for her seaplanes. Wherever there were good level stretches of land she built fields for her landplanes. The islands under her mandate became literally floating fortresses.

It is because of her strength in those islands that it was never possible to send assistance to the defenders of Bataan Peninsula or Corregidor. It is because of her strength in those islands that Japan has been able to extend her lines of communication safely far southward of the Equator. On the islands themselves she based scouting and bombing planes. Submarines and fast cruisers patrolled in perfect safety behind and west of the islands, ready to sail out and attack as soon as the scouting planes might report the approach of attackers. Safe, deep passages between the islands are few and are heavily mined. To have sent a battle fleet and transports to try to crash through that chain of floating fortresses would have been a suicidal gamble, with the odds heavily against the attackers.

Although the United States has disavowed any intention of territorial expansion at the end of the war, these islands obviously must be taken away from Japan, and it seems equally obvious that they should belong to the United States. If we hold the islands Japan now controls we shall always be assured of safe access to the Philippines for both ships and planes, and from the Philippines to China the distance is only 460 miles. Certainly if the Philippines choose outright independence we must be in a position to protect them from any menace to their safety that may arise, and it will also be essential that we are never again cut off from maritime or aerial contact with our ally, China.

The only satisfactory alternative to outright annexation of these islands by the United States would be to have them under control of some international organization strong enough to protect them from attack or aggression. They will be important as ports to the aerial argosies of the near future, and, whether we own the islands outright or not, all landing and fueling facilities for the air lines of the future should be accessible on equal terms to the commercial planes of all nations, just as the Panama Canal was open to the world's ships in the years of peace.

Hawaii, the Marshalls, the Carolines, Guam, and the Philippines will lie along one of the world's greatest com-

mercial air lanes of the future. Whatever disposition is made
of the islands westward of Hawaii, it will be essential that
they are not in weak hands.

Second in importance to the Marshalls and the Carolines,
with their air stations on the route to East Asia, will be the
strings and groups of islands stretching southwestward to
New Zealand and Australia. Some of them belong to the
United States, some to Britain, some to France, and some
are mandated to the two great British dominions with
which we shall have increasingly important cultural and
economic relationships after the war.

International control of this great aerial route would also
be in the interests of the unfettered growth of communica-
tions. Before the attack on Pearl Harbor ridiculous conditions existed in this area. The great Clipper planes were
forced to maintain their southwest terminus at Auckland,
in New Zealand. Australia would not let them land on the
Australian continent because the American Government
would not grant Australian operators the right to use
Hawaii as a landing point for an air line projected from
Sydney to Vancouver, British Columbia.

Even under the urgency of perilous conditions created
by the growing certainty of war these restrictions were
maintained by both sides until after December 7, 1941. The
result was that Auckland was a serious bottleneck, and
scores of passengers who landed at Auckland from the
Clippers were forced to wait there for weeks before they

could get across the 1,200 miles of the Tasman Sea to Australia.

Americans going to China on official missions—military men, diplomats, high naval officers, men with important war-production contracts—were unconscionably delayed at Auckland. There were literally no passenger ships running between New Zealand and Australia, and the smaller seaplanes which carried passengers and mail between Auckland and Sydney made at most three round trips every fortnight. Less than two months before the attack on Pearl Harbor more than seventy Americans, Britons, Australians, Chinese, and Netherlanders from the East Indies, men bound on war missions of extreme importance, were indefinitely delayed in Auckland because Clipper planes could not touch at Australian ports.

The American refusal to permit Australian air lines to land at Hawaii was particularly absurd, for if the permission had been granted it would have been merely a paper proceeding. Australia was so short of airplanes that the proposed line could not possibly have begun operations until after the end of the war.

France will probably offer the greatest resistance and the most numerous objections to pooling her Pacific islands under some form of international administration; and yet the French islands have been the most inefficiently and corruptly administered of all these small holdings, except those ruled by Japan, just as French Indo-China was the white man's most discreditable colonial outpost on the Asiatic mainland.

France owned part of the New Hebrides group, New Caledonia (used as a penal colony), the Loyalty Islands, the Marquesas, the Tuomatu Archipelago, the Tubuai or Austral Islands, and the Society Islands, which include famous Tahiti. Papeete, the Tahitian capital, was the governmental headquarters of all these scattered French holdings. The semicomic but disgraceful conflict for control at Papeete which followed the collapse of France will someday afford material for a sardonic sketch of how the white man sometimes misbehaves in far places.

Except for the indisputable fact of China's just claim for the return of Formosa, this great island would automatically become the western terminus of the great chain of island steppingstones leading westward across the Pacific from Hawaii to the eastern coast of the Asiatic mainland. Already Formosa has magnificent airports, developed by the Japanese, and this island is only a little more than 100 miles from the China coast.

Formosa, renamed Taiwan by the Japanese, was ceded to Japan under the Treaty of Shimonoseki in 1895, but actually the transfer was made only on paper on a Japanese warship. China had lost the war, but the Formosans would permit neither Peking's representative nor the Japanese to land. The Japanese acquisition of Formosa was really made by military conquest, for the Formosans declared a republic, and it required five months of fighting before Japan was able to establish authority. There have been frequent rebellions during the whole period of Japanese occupation.

Formosa has an area of 13,807 square miles, which is about equal to the combined areas of Massachusetts, Connecticut, and Rhode Island. When the Japanese came into control the Chinese population was estimated at 2,600,000; today it has grown to more than 5,000,000. In 1895 the island's main exports were rice, sugar, tea, and camphor, and these items still made up 75 per cent of Formosa's exports in 1938, the latest year for which official figures are obtainable.

Formosa's trade development shows clearly the Japanese method with annexed or conquered territories, and the figures are valuable because the same process has been under way in Manchuria for a decade and in the occupied portions of China since 1937. Before Japan grabbed the island 63 per cent of all exports went to China, but in 1938 the total was only 1.7 per cent. In 1895 China furnished 37.4 per cent of all Formosan imports; by 1938 this had dwindled to 0.5 per cent. In former years the United States furnished 5.3 per cent of all imports, and Great Britain 7.3 per cent. In 1938 imports from the United States were 0.4 per cent, and Britain's share was down to zero. By 1938 Japan furnished 89.4 per cent of all Formosan imports, and Japan, Korea, and Manchuria took 97.8 per cent of all exports.

This remarkable turnover of the economic life of the

island was not accomplished only by including Formosa in Japan's tariff system. Camphor, salt, tobacco, and opium were made Japanese Government monopolies, tax discriminations were employed against all foreign exporters and importers, and Japanese steamship companies, which controlled all of the island's trade, charged foreign firms double the freight rates paid by Japanese concerns. In an effort to sever all ties between the Formosan people and China, Japan forbade immigration and emigration and relaxed these rulings only for the seasonal importation of an average of 10,000 Chinese coolie laborers from the mainland.

Formosa offers an excellent example of the unwillingness of the Japanese to emigrate, even though they seek to justify their policy of territorial expansion on the plea of overpopulation. During the forty-seven years of Japanese control, while the native population of the islands has about doubled—from 2,600,000 to more than 5,000,000—the Japanese population of Formosa reached a peak of only 309,000 in 1938, or less than 5.5 per cent of the whole.

Indictments of Japan as a colonial power become monotonous because of the necessity for reiteration. In Formosa the usual policies were followed. Only the Japanese language was taught in the schools, and police regulations governed even native religious, marriage, and burial ceremonies. Spies and informers have swarmed in the island for decades, and the people were so resentful and rebellious-minded that in 1938 it was necessary to maintain one Japanese policeman for every 580 Formosans. In Japan, in the same year, the percentage was one policeman to every 1,052 Japanese civilians.

Formosa will offer no problem involving future autonomy or independence, as will Korea, the Philippines, and the Netherlands East Indies, and since the population is overwhelmingly Chinese in blood and in language, Formosa should not be included in any international arrangement that may be made for most of the Pacific islands, but should become at once an integral part of China. Here, too, as in Korea and Manchuria, Japan's economic hold must be entirely severed, and if the Japanese who reside there are not repatriated they will be subjected to persecution and assassination by the people whom they have abused and oppressed for nearly half a century. No local administration would be strong enough to provide them with adequate protection.

No matter what kind of peace is finally made, it will be necessary to assure that the peace is upheld by power—not by potential power but by actual power—and this actual power must be in hands that will not scruple to use it if an emergency or a threat arises.

The people of the United States may as well reconcile themselves to the fact that at the end of this war the very circumstances of their existence and the geographical location of their country will force upon them a role of power —probably the greatest power existing in the world, when hostilities cease—and it will be more important to exercise this power in the Far Pacific than across the Atlantic.

It is unthinkable that they will use this power in the outdated and discredited manner of the old imperialisms. Even if all the victor nations should be willing to abrogate enough of their individual sovereign rights to create a great international authority with paramount power on the globe, it would still be the United States which would have to give that international authority most of its weight and strength, and it would be Washington which would play a predominant role in all decisions reached. This will be necessary because power brings responsibility, and if responsibility is shirked, power dwindles away and finally vanishes.

There was ample potential power to enforce the Treaty of Versailles, or to amend it as justice dictated, but the nations concerned would not wield that power, either individually or collectively. If this country and the other United Nations which emerge victors from this war shirk responsibility and fail to find a way to use their power to enforce peace and bring the promised four freedoms to the peoples of the world, then the present holocaust will prove to have been as senseless and as useless as was the struggle waged from 1914 to 1918.

Even before this war started, the most remote of the Pacific islands was only five days' flight from San Francisco. At the end of the war, airplane improvements will probably bring the most remote to within forty hours' flying range.

At the end of the war those islands should be disarmed and placed under some international policing and administrative authority, and those now fortified into floating fortresses should be made steppingstones for commerce across the greatest of the world's oceans.

CHAPTER XVII

Matsuoka in Reserve

J APAN, while fighting desperately for victory, is also planning far ahead to save what she can if she meets a decisive
defeat. In the United States her agents are misleading pro-
pacifist elements in a movement favoring a soft peace, and
in Japan itself *the Empire's ablest diplomats and bargainers
are being kept in eclipse in order that they may be later
pushed into the foreground as representing "liberal
thought" when the time comes for a defeated Japan to try
for a peace settlement* which will permit the Japanese to
retain at least a portion of what they have stolen.

The ablest of all the diplomats being held in reserve—and
the one most dangerous to the United States because he
lived long in this country and knows how we think and
feel—is Yosuke Matsuoka, who was Japan's Foreign Min-

ister in Prince Konoye's third Cabinet and resigned in the summer of 1941 soon after Hitler attacked the Soviets.

Matsuoka, once pro-American, was the Foreign Minister who reversed his attitude so basically as to become one of the leaders of the "anti-white man" clique in Japan, and who engineered his country into joining the German-Italian Axis in September 1940. In the spring of 1941 Matsuoka made a tour to Berlin and Rome, conferred at length with Hitler and Mussolini, and stopped off in Moscow for a week on his way homeward. During this visit he negotiated the neutrality pact between his country and the Soviet Union and was greeted as a conquering hero when he returned to Tokyo. However, within a few weeks he retired in disgrace, for Hitler, after encouraging Matsuoka to make a deal with Stalin, "lost face" for the Japanese Foreign Minister by his surprise attack on the Soviet Union.

To the Occidental, Matsuoka's having led Japan into joining the Axis would seem to bar him from taking a major part in the eventual peace parleys. But the Japanese, being Orientals, do not think or reason as we do. The Japanese will doubtless advance Matsuoka as their ideal spokesman at the peace table, pretending that since Hitler once "betrayed" him he has seen the error of his ways and has again become ardently pro-American in his principles.

During my fifteen years in the Far East, I ranked Matsuoka second amongst the five men whom I considered my closest Japanese friends. I admired his ability and his agile mind more than I admired any Japanese. I watched his rapid climb from comparative obscurity as one of several vice-presidents of the South Manchuria Railway, Tokyo's great financial weapon of imperialist expansion. He led Japan's delegation out of the League of Nations when, after long hearings in Geneva, the League condemned the Empire's aggressions in Manchuria. Then came for him one of those periods of retirement into obscurity which are seemingly an integral part of every political career in Japan.

Matsuoka emerged as managing president of the South Manchuria Railway and became reconciled with the expansionist clique in the Japanese Army. After a brilliant career as head of the great railway system, Matsuoka again experienced a period of retirement, only to appear as Foreign Minister and a strong candidate for the premiership. Now again he is in retirement, but his re-emergence is certain and must be regarded with caution by the United States. He is now bitterly anti-American and anti-British, and his exceptional abilities make him exceptionally dangerous.

Yosuke Matsuoka's convictions shift and change, but he himself is unalterably two things—he is always pro-Japanese and pro-Matsuoka. He has alternately reviled the militarists and then done their bidding slavishly and led the chorus of banzais over their achievements. He has been the chosen head of conservative capitalism in his business and public life, while at the same time nursing personal convictions and patterning his personal affairs along lines which in Japan would be termed radical. He has been equally enthusiastic as a reasoning apostle of peace and as a frothing advocate of war.

Japan has coveted eastern Siberia for more than two decades, and this passion for possession is based upon strategic, economic, and political considerations of the greatest weight. To the Japanese the continuance of Vladivostok under other than Japan's ownership constitutes "a pistol pointed at the heart of the Empire," as countless generals, admirals, and Cabinet members are never tired of telling the Japanese people. Japan covets Siberia's oil resources, fisheries, forests, farm lands, and the wide range of existing mineral reserves. In addition Japan fears the influence of the proximity of the Soviets upon 60,000,000 discontented Koreans and Manchurians now held in unwilling subjugation.

Japan has already made two attempts to get eastern Siberia. The first, known to all the world, occurred from 1918 to 1922, when her armies occupied vast areas and finally withdrew under pressure from Washington and after a series of disastrous conflicts with Russian guerrillas. The other attempt was made in secret in the early part of November 1938, by Matsuoka, then president of the South Manchuria Railway.

Matsuoka chose me as intermediary in his secret move in

the autumn of 1938, and at his instigation I forwarded to the White House a series of astounding proposals for the acquisition of eastern Siberia and for what he termed "a community of interest between Japan and the United States." His proposal sought to drag the United States into a perilous imperialistic expansion upon the Asiatic mainland and to induce President Roosevelt to commit the American Government to the greatest territorial purchase in the history of the world.

Later he became a professed jingo, became anti-American and even "anti-white man," but in 1938 Matsuoka deplored and denounced the policies of the Japanese militarists and said he was even ready to withdraw Japan's armies from most of China if only President Roosevelt would accept his audacious proposals.

Yosuke Matsuoka will no doubt reappear in Japanese political life; all Japanese politicians do so. He may again become Foreign Minister and may even become Premier, and Japan will certainly try to get him a seat at the peace table, if there is a negotiated peace. He wanted to be Prime Minister in 1938 and said he would achieve that office if our President accepted his plans for acquiring eastern Siberia. Indeed, the cold reception given to his scheme at the White House and the consequent frustration of his ambition may have contributed largely to his shift from a pro-American attitude to that of one of the bitterest enemies this country has in Japan.

Matsuoka chose me as intermediary to handle his secret proposals to President Roosevelt because we had then been good friends for a decade. I had known him when he was vice-president of the South Manchuria Railway, had conferred with him often during his period of temporary eclipse after he led the Japanese delegation out of the League of Nations, and saw him often when he later became president of the railway. During this latter period he confessed to me over brandy and black coffee one night that I had saved his life without knowing that I was doing so. I was blankly incredulous.

"Don't you remember one night in February 1932, when we were fighting the Chinese in Shanghai?" he asked. "I telephoned and asked if we might dine together, so that I could outline to you my plans for ending that Shanghai battle, and wanted you to discuss my plan with the American admiral and consul general. Remember now?"

I remembered very well. Over the telephone I had agreed to the dinner proposal and asked Matsuoka where I should join him—in the lobby of the Cathay Hotel or in his private sitting room? To my surprise he replied: "I think I had better come to you, to your apartment. Will you feed a hungry man?"

There were reasons for my misgivings about the success of that party. My Chinese cook was so anti-Japanese in his feelings that he had taken a small nail and driven a hole in each can of an eighty-dollar purchase of Japanese tinned seafood I had bought not long before, just so the contents would spoil. But Matsuoka came, the dinner was good, and his peace proposals were interesting but impractical and led to nothing.

"Well, the night of that dinner I was to have been assassinated by Japanese ruffians because of my peace efforts," he confided to me years later. "I had to get out of my hotel secretly by using an elevator reserved for servants. You may remember that while I was actually in hiding in your apartment I received a telephone call. That was to let me know that the plotters had all been arrested. By feeding me that night, you helped to save my life."

This man Yosuke Matsuoka is an unstable dreamer of great dreams, but his loyalties (except to Matsuoka) are not constant. He can be a stern realist up to a point, and then his emotions and prejudices blind him to realities. Short and thickset, with a round, boyish face in spite of his sixty-two years, Matsuoka wears a mustache which is bristlingly military but which is counteracted by his ready and genial smile. He is a good listener, but he likes to talk a lot, and he lets the sound of his own voice and the ready roll of his well-chosen words carry him away. He confesses that because much of his boyhood was spent in the United States he likes to think in English, but that after "a few drinks" he reverts to type and can think only in Japanese.

Japan's future Foreign Minister landed in Portland, Oregon, in 1893, at the age of thirteen, and was almost penniless. He worked his way through school in Portland and then went to high school in Oakland, California. Later he went through the law school of the University of Oregon and when he was twenty years of age received his LL.B. Ambitious, thrifty, hard-working, he found no job too humble to help him on his way. He waited on table, was a bus boy, labored as a field hand in Japanese-owned truck gardens, and for a time was even a house servant.

Some people who do not know him well believe his anti-Americanism is based upon some slights he experienced during these early years—slights based upon racial prejudices. This is incorrect. His anti-Americanism dates from the period when President Roosevelt rejected the secret proposals for American-Japanese partnership which he asked me to transmit. Before his plans were rejected by the White House, Matsuoka often said to me:

"Oregon is the most beautiful place in the world. If, when I am old and tired, our Emperor thinks I deserve well of my country, nothing could make me happier than to be given an honorable retirement by being appointed our consul general at Portland."

Matsuoka is a peculiar type of man to have long held the position of president of the South Manchuria Railway, which for years was the active agent of Japan's preparatory imperialism in Manchuria. Although he had every opportunity to become one of Japan's notable multimillionaires, he has never chosen to amass great wealth.

"I'd be an outlaw if people on the inside knew my convictions," he told me one evening at Dairen. "Here I am, holding one of the greatest positions in the gift of an imperialistic and capitalistic state. And yet I have no faith in either the more violent forms of imperialism or in capitalism. I'm no millionaire, but I'm a fairly rich man, and yet my sons know they will inherit nothing when I die. They have each had the best education I could afford for them, but even that hurt my social conscience, for why should my sons, just because they are *my* sons, have a better education than the sons of a peasant or a laborer? Upon graduation each boy was given 1,500 yen and told that he must make his own way. When I die, if my wife survives me, she will have a modest income from a trust fund, but the rest of my fortune will be willed to the nation."

Toward China, Matsuoka's attitude, until he became Foreign Minister with the backing of the jingo militarists, was always kind and benevolent, but tinged with patronage and a sense of superiority. And that is just the attitude which the Chinese justly resent and which has for four decades made impossible any real friendship between the two countries.

Late in August of 1936, less than a year before the terrible and protracted Sino-Japanese hostilities began, I arrived at Dairen one day at noon by ship from Shanghai. At my hotel I found awaiting me a still-treasured note from Matsuoka:

DEAR ABEND:

There's no decent foreign food to be had in this city, and all the Japanese cooks are terrible. But in my house at the beach I have what is probably the best Chinese cook in all Manchuria. Shall we have Chinese chow at 7, with a dozen or so of my friends who wish to meet you? If possible, come about 5, and we can have a quiet talk before the mob arrives—Yrs.— Y. MATSUOKA.

Soon after five I was there. His house, halfway up the hill, overlooked the graceful curve of Hoshigaura Beach. Southward were precipitous and tawny-colored islands rearing from the blue waters of the Gulf of Chihli. It was like a bit of the western Italian coast, just south of Genoa, in coloring and in beauty.

With whisky sodas at our elbows and our feet on the veranda railing, Matsuoka and I sat and talked and drank, and sometimes just smoked in easy silence, while the sunset flared and paled and died, and the first stars came out.

"Our damned war dogs are straining again to get at China's throat," said Matsuoka, after an unusually long silence. "Those poor Chinese—they need our friendship, not our hate nor our force. And they will never love us while we hold bayonets at their throats.

"The Yellow River is on rampage again," he continued,

with a southward sweep of one hand, "and again justifying its name of China's Sorrow. A couple of hours away over that opal-tinted sea is Shantung province, with more than 35,000,000 oppressed and poverty-stricken people—half the population of Japan, that would be. But what is being done for them? They are trying to stem that terrible flood with bundles of dry branches and wheelbarrow loads of rock and clay. That is all only a symbol. It is Japan's destiny to help those hapless people. Instead of bundles of faggots and wheelbarrows, we must go in there with modern American dredging machinery, curb that devilish river, and make the fields and crops and lives of those thirty-odd million peasants safe."

Japan "went in" to Shantung, and with a vengeance. Japanese airplanes bombed Shantung cities. Japanese soldiers killed those Shantung peasants by the tens of thousands, looted their villages, and raped their women. Farther to the west, in another province, Japanese soldiers cut the dikes of that same river over which Matsuoka sentimentalized, and less than two years later they flooded vast farming areas so thoroughly that part of the stream has changed its course, and an area larger than some of our Atlantic seaboard states has been ruined by sandy silt for several generations.

Some powerful influence—possibly ambition—changed the benevolent Matsuoka into a fire-breathing mouthpiece for the Japanese military clique, and he now joins them in declaring that China must be "subjugated" and that the

Chinese Government must be "destroyed." Can he have forgotten his own beliefs of six years ago? "They need our friendship . . . they will never love us while we hold bayonets at their throats."

This strange and unstable man, who cherished a fantastic plan concerning Japanese-American relations, but who would have changed the history of the last two years had his plan been possible of achievement, had an admirable background for his tasks when he became Foreign Minister of Japan.

After spending nine of his most formative years in Oregon and California, he returned to Japan at the age of twenty-two, studied the Japanese and Chinese classics and international law for two years, and then entered upon what was to be an eighteen-year career in diplomacy. He was in the consulate general at Shanghai, was private secretary to Count Shimpei Goto when that nobleman held the Foreign Office portfolio, and was also secretary to Premier Takashi Hara. In 1919 he was one of Japan's important delegates at the Paris Peace Conference.

The next year, 1920, Matsuoka quit the diplomatic service, but soon became one of the directors of the South Manchuria Railway, then its vice-president, and finally president of that gigantic concern. In 1931, when he went to Geneva to plead Japan's case when the Lytton Commission's report on Manchuria was being considered, he startled but did not convince the delegates by his fiery impromptu speeches. When more than two-score nations voted against Japan, he announced the Empire's formal withdrawal from the League and then went home by way of the United States, making blustering and angry speeches en route.

When Matsuoka made his astonishing proposal to President Roosevelt in the early winter of 1938, he was still president of the South Manchuria Railway, but confided to me then that he intended to resign early in 1939, and he did so. If his proposal to the United States was even cordially received, he said, he would probably be the next Premier of Japan. It was evident, even then, that Prince Konoye's Cabinet would soon resign, and Matsuoka told me that if he himself was not the next Premier probably Baron Hiranuma would assume the office. Matsuoka was then so high in the councils of inner government that his proposals about Siberia must have had the approval of even the Emperor himself.

True to his prophecy, the Government resigned early in 1939, and Hiranuma formed a short-lived Cabinet which fell in the autumn of that same year because of the Hitler-Stalin pact made just before the war began in Europe. Hiranuma had been a stanch advocate of an alliance with Germany, and when Hitler chummed up with Stalin, then considered Japan's worst foe, Hiranuma retired in a confusion of "lost face" equaled only subsequently by Matsuoka's own shelving. But there is no permanent retirement for men of this stripe in Japan. Baron Hiranuma was back in office in Prince Konoye's Cabinet which resigned in July of 1941 and is again an influential member of the Tojo regime. Matsuoka is almost certain to return to high office in similar fashion.

Matsuoka was suggested as Hiranuma's successor as Premier in the autumn of 1939, but did not want the job then. When General Abe organized his short-lived Cabinet there was much talk of appointing Matsuoka as Japan's ambassador to Washington, but he did not want that post either. He dislikes failure and could see no successes possible for any ambassador from Tokyo in view of the fact that his "community of interest" proposals had fallen flat.

It was late in October of 1938 that I began to plan a trip from Shanghai through Manchukuo and North China to survey the situation for the New York *Times*. As always, before going to Dairen or Mukden, I called upon Matsuoka's personal representative in Shanghai to find out when his chief, then president of the great railway, would be in Manchukuo. Contact with Matsuoka was always of prime news importance. I learned that he was then in Japan, but would fly back to Dairen about November 6.

On November 7 I sailed from Shanghai for Dairen, and I reached that seaport city about noon on the ninth. On the afternoon of that day I spent about an hour with Matsuoka in his office, and we talked of everything from Chamberlain's Munich agreement to the then recent capture of Canton by the Japanese Army. On the morning of the tenth we both left Dairen by train, northbound for Mukden, and I made part of the journey in Matsuoka's private compartment.

He talked with his customary frankness of all aspects of the Far Eastern situation, and yet I was conscious of some reserve or preoccupation. Cordiality was not lacking, and yet I felt that I was being barred from some idea that occupied half of his mind.

We alighted from the train at Mukden at about midday. A subzero wind, gritty with dust from the Gobi Desert so thick that it gave the sunlight the color of dirty tan, was sweeping the station platform. After a few words in Japanese with a group of dignitaries who awaited his arrival, Matsuoka asked me to dine with him that night at the Yamato Hotel.

The dinner was a success; yet I knew that something vital was being withheld. The other guests were three vice-presidents of the South Manchuria Railway and four other Japanese whose names and rank I cannot recall. Matsuoka did not lead the talk, but often drummed abstractedly with his fingers, rolled pellets of bread, and then suddenly barged into the conversation with questions which showed his previous inattention.

We broke up a little before midnight, and Matsuoka said good-by. He was leaving for Korea by the noon train, he said, and we would probably not meet again until my next trip to Manchukuo. He laughed off my suggestion that he come to Shanghai and investigate the many grievances against Japanese military conduct and restrictions which Americans and Europeans were then nursing. I said good-by with reluctance and with a lively sense that, for some reason, I had failed to establish that degree of intimate contact necessary to learning what was in the back of Matsuoka's mind.

Up in my room I made ready for bed, and then gingerly opened the double windows a narrow crack. The wind had died away; there was no gritty dust in the air, and all the stars seemed to be working with overtime brilliancy, while the temperature was dropping like a sounding lead in a calm sea. Assured that the dust storm had subsided, I flung the windows wide and made a shivering dive for bed—and the telephone jangled.

"Hello!" I bellowed, none too courteously, for I was shaking with cold and felt sure that the ring, at that time of night, would bring only the operator's apologetic and all too frequent "Mushi-mushi? Wrong number." But no, it was Matsuoka's warm and friendly voice.

"I'd like to see you again," he said. "Something important. Will you come to my sitting room here in the hotel at 9 tomorrow morning and keep your time clear until at least 10:30 o'clock?"

Sleep was slow in coming that night, for my mind was busy with conjectures. Was Matsuoka going to tell me of a gigantic plan for railway extension from Manchukuo into the occupied regions of North China? Was the Japanese Army forcing him out of office, perhaps, because he would not always do their bidding? At dinner he had laughingly said that the Army apparently knew more about railroading than he knew; that they had forced him to build half a score of new strategic northern lines pointing to the Siberian border, and that to his amazement each line had made money from the day it was opened. Was the long-deferred outbreak of large-scale hostilities along the Manchukuo-Siberian border about to take place? But all these conjectures were wide of the mark, both in scope and in subject, from the plan which Matsuoka wanted me to transmit to the White House.

Next morning he began by saying that he had read or heard that the initial proposals for what resulted in the Washington Conference in 1921–22 had originated in Downing Street with the British and that the late Adolph Ochs, then publisher of the New York *Times*, transmitted the suggestions from the British Foreign Office to President Harding and Secretary of State Hughes.

"I am now asking you to ask your present publisher, Mr. Arthur Hays Sulzberger, to forward my suggestions direct to President Roosevelt," Matsuoka continued. "Except for the President, Secretary Hull, and Mr. Sulzberger, no one in America must know of this proposal or that it comes from me. If the plan seemed to originate in Japanese circles it would have less chance of success. I have specific and important reasons for not using our embassy in Washington to transmit this idea. If you will write to Mr. Sulzberger, I could send the letter to Yokohama by a personal courier for mailing aboard an American or British steamer, but I prefer to have you get it out through Hongkong, where there is no chance of interference or of censorship."

At that time, about ten months before the beginning of the second World War, Hongkong had no censorship, but in Japan and in Manchukuo all mails were rigidly censored, as were all mails posted in Shanghai or elsewhere in China where the Japanese Army was in control. Matsuoka said that if "certain elements" in the Japanese Army learned of his proposals, which would set aside many military plans in China and for southward expansion, both his life and my own would probably be forfeit.

The final arrangement agreed upon was that after Matsuoka had approved of my detailed notes of our conversation, which he did in writing later that day, November 11, I was to keep those notes on my person night and day until I got back to Shanghai and then recast the notes into letter form for President Roosevelt and Secretary Hull. This I did on November 28, making three copies, one of which I still retain. The other two were handed to F. Tillman Durdin, then the Chungking correspondent of the New York *Times,* who had been covering Shanghai news for me while I was on my trip north.

Durdin, who to this day has no idea what the letters contained, was instructed to have them locked in the safe by the purser of the American ship by which he traveled, to take them out of the safe only after the ship had docked at Hongkong, and then to put one copy aboard a Clipper plane about to depart for Manila and San Francisco and to mail the second copy aboard a Canadian Pacific "Empress" liner about to sail for Vancouver, B.C.

Both letters were addressed to Mr. Sulzberger, with the request that he acknowledge the receipt of each one by cable and that he indicate in his first cable whether he would be willing to send or take Matsuoka's astounding proposal to President Roosevelt. These elaborate and rather stagy precautions were taken at the earnest insistence of Mr. Matsuoka, who was heartily afraid of detection by Japanese censors or spies and who was also apprehensive lest any of the secret agents of one of the European Powers, who then swarmed all over the Far East, should learn of his bold project. Most of the text of the letter, as finally sent, consisted of direct approved quotes from Mr. Matsuoka.

Had I been a fingernail biter, I'd have gnawed down to the quick before all these details were arranged, for as yet Matsuoka had given no inkling of what he had to propose. Finally, lighting a much-too-strong cigar, closing all the doors to his sitting room, and instructing the telephone exchange that he was not to be disturbed, he began a succinct and businesslike explanation.

"You see, Abend, I am afraid we are drifting toward

another World War, and what I am suggesting is at once a measure of appeasement toward certain parties, as well as a measure insuring Japan against having to fight against either Soviet Russia or the United States. I want to remove the menace to Japan of Soviet planes from Vladivostok and of Soviet armies from the Manchukuo and Korean frontiers, and at the same time achieve a real community of interest with the United States. So I propose a mutually profitable business deal—a gigantic land purchase.

"I am referring to eastern Siberia; not alone to the Maritime Provinces, but to all of eastern Siberia east of Lake Baikal. Japan can no longer live under the constant threat of the vast Russian armies maintained there, the 80 submarines at Vladivostok, the 700 airplanes along our northern borders in Manchukuo, with another 900 Soviet planes on call only twenty-four hours away.

"If this situation is not amended within a short time, our Army will strike. Nothing will check our chauvinists except the personal interference of our Emperor, and that would be difficult. The clash cannot be averted longer than three years, and I fear it may come much earlier and with lightning suddenness. A war of this kind will mean a World War, and under present tendencies America would eventually become Japan's foe. I would avoid that if it were humanly possible. For us to fight the United States would be national hara-kiri."

Six months after Matsuoka made this prophecy, actual

large-scale warfare broke out between Japan and Russia in the Nomonhan area on the borders of Manchukuo and Outer Mongolia. Japan officially admitted 18,000 Japanese soldiers killed and wounded, and each side claimed to have shot down several hundred of the enemy's airplanes. Only Japan's suggestions for an armistice, made in the fall of 1939 when Russia began her invasion of Poland, brought the fighting to an end. It had been going on from June to mid-September.

At this point in his proposals Matsuoka made a long digression, dealing with the lack of discipline and the "spirit of defiance" in the Japanese Army. Admiration of German military methods had brought Japan to a sad pass, he declared, and he feared the development within the Empire "of something as evil as Hitlerism" unless Japan could form a partnership with the United States.

"What I propose is that the United States and Japan make an offer for the joint purchase of all of Siberia east of Lake Baikal. Thirty billion yen might swing the deal, but if necessary fifty billion could be invested, with a down payment of ten billion yen and the rest spread over the next thirty years. Each nation could jointly guarantee the other, if Stalin should make such a demand."

Matsuoka agreed with me when I interrupted and said there would be difficulties, especially in Congress. He argued that the United States had often before purchased territories, and not always with Congressional consent. He cited the Louisiana Purchase, Florida, Alaska, the Philippine Islands, the Virgin Islands. And he emphasized that he was not proposing any kind of an "entangling alliance," which our traditions forbid, but merely a business partnership.

"The area I have in mind is a little more than 1,000,000 square miles in extent," he said, lighting his second cigar and spreading a huge map on the floor between us. "This northern half," he leaned forward and pointed with a pencil, "is mostly quaking tundra, with some important forests. The other half, larger than Manchuria, is agricultural land as magnificent as much of Canada. It has forests, fresh- and salt-water fisheries, coal, iron, gold, and here in Kamchatka there is probably oil.

"This enormous area has a civilian population of less than 2,000,000, and of this total more than 800,000 are exiled Cossacks and Ukrainians. They would welcome a change of masters. They hate Moscow and have a secret organization working for autonomy. They maintain headquarters in Harbin, which we wink at, for we know all about their moves and aspirations. The habitable and tillable area of eastern Siberia, larger than Manchuria, could easily support an equally large population, and Manchukuo now has nearly 35,000,000 people."

Matsuoka then went into considerable detail about securing safety for Japan. "I have it in mind," he said, "that if this purchase can be made, Washington, Tokyo, and Moscow can reach an agreement for the complete demilitariza-

tion of the new border. This whole line, from Lake Baikal
northward and southward, should be as free of forts and of
soldiers as is the American-Canadian boundary."

Consulting the text of my letter, written for President
Roosevelt to read, I find the following amplification of Matsuoka's plan for handling this huge area if the purchase deal
could have been concluded. Quoting Matsuoka, I wrote:

America and Japan could jointly furnish a small force of
gendarmes for policing the purchased area, or Japan alone
could furnish such a force, with American observers and advisers. Such details could easily be adjusted, once the basic
principle of partnership is accepted.

All of Siberia suffers from the lack of year-round ice-free
seaports. We could build north-south railways and highways,
draining the production southward through Manchurian and
Korean harbors, and could, moreover, jointly guarantee Russia
through traffic rights for the import and export of goods for
all the region east of the Ural Mountains.

Matsuoka's exposition of the situation, designed for the
White House, continued:

I look at it this way: Japan must remove the Russian menace
from eastern Siberia. To do it by warfare would cost thirty or
forty billion yen, besides the enormous cost in lives and properties on both sides—and the practical certainty of a European
involvement, a World War, and American embroilment against
Japan as well.

It seems to me to be wise statesmanship and economics to

buy this area, with America as partner, and so save the destruction of lives and properties and the squandering of wealth. A
partnership of this kind would also put an end to the American-
Japanese naval building competition. And it would bring great
wealth to both purchasers within the next quarter century.
Problems of exploitation, investment, immigration, and administration could be easily solved in fairness to both sides.

This is the end of the portion of the letter consisting of
direct quotation from Mr. Matsuoka. But, writing to Mr.
Sulzberger, I continued the letter as follows:

When Matsuoka asked for my opinion, I told him I thought
it was a wild scheme, and with brutal frankness I said I thought
it had not a chance of success. He asked why I adopted such a
pessimistic view, and I told him:

First, in view of Japan's flouting of treaties in Manchuria and
in China, and in view of the present continuous encroachment
upon foreign rights, I believe the American public would not
consider Japan as an honest or a reliable partner. He then
intimated that if such a deal can be put through, Japan will be
prepared to observe the Open Door scrupulously in China.

More than that, Matsuoka said that if he became Foreign
Minister or Premier he would arrange to have the Japanese
Army withdraw from South China and from the Yangtsze
Valley as well. I then mentioned Shantung province, and
he said Japan would evacuate that area, too, but only reluctantly, as the price of securing American adhesion to the
land-purchase plan in eastern Siberia.

But when the question of North China was broached, he was stubborn. Japan would not and could not, he said, ever move out of the provinces of Hopeh, Shansi, Charhar, and Suiyuan. In other words they want to keep the Peiping-Tientsin area, the coal mines of Shansi, the railway which runs through what was Inner Mongolia and which now traverses Charhar and Suiyuan, as well as the coal and iron deposits of that region. Most of all, Japan wants to retain a military foothold along the southern flank of Soviet-dominated Outer Mongolia.

Reverting again to my letter to Mr. Sulzberger:

Second, I told Matsuoka that such a purchase deal would crack the Tokyo-Berlin-Rome anti-Comintern Axis. He seemed not to understand, whereupon I told him that Hitler, in particular, would be aghast at having Russia come into a lump sum of ten billion yen and would be even more aghast at the demilitarization of the Soviet's eastern borders, thus permitting Stalin to transfer his huge Siberian army and large air force to the Soviet European frontiers.

This was at a period when Hitler was denouncing the Soviet and Communism as the enemies of mankind, and about nine months before Berlin and Moscow made the agreement, in August of 1939, which gave Hitler a free hand to fight England and France.

This aspect of the proposition seemed momentarily almost to stun Matsuoka. He admitted frankly that he had not considered that angle of the deal. He had, however, thought it over in detail in relation to England and France and believed that both would acquiesce with good grace, on the theory that Japan's restless expansionism would be busied for many decades in eastern Siberia and that as a result the "push to the southwest" would first be eased and then soon ended.

After thinking deeply and in immobile silence for a few minutes, Matsuoka brightened. "We can and will appease Hitler," he said. "I know a way. Set your mind at rest on that point." But he offered no explanation, and in view of the long list of perfidies to which he committed Japan after becoming Minister of Foreign Affairs, I wonder what he may have had in mind.

Amongst other persuasive arguments which Matsuoka used to me that day in November 1938, when he placed his ambitious proposals before me, was that Russia would probably take part payment from the United States in goods, foods, and machinery. Japan's factories were then all busy making war materials, he said, wherefore American business would profit immensely from the barter; and unemployment, then serious in the United States, would take a sharp drop.

It was, of course, never possible for the American Government to consider any kind of proposal which would betray China to the extent of leaving Japan in possession of four provinces in North China. But had such an agreement been within the range of practical politics, the history of the world would have been profoundly changed.

Had Stalin been able to secure ten billion yen in a lump sum and to transfer his Siberian forces to the Russian European front, he would probably never have made that pact with Hitler in 1939 which left Germany free to fight only on the west after Poland was vanquished. And today there would probably not be a victorious Japanese army of occupation in the Philippines, Indo-China, Siam, Burma, the Netherlands East Indies, British Malaya, and Singapore.

Matsuoka's proposals were taken secretly to President Roosevelt early in 1939 by Mr. Sulzberger. They created a sensation in inner circles of the administration and State Department. There is no question but that up to that time, and for the preceding decade, Matsuoka had been intensely pro-American. His declaration in the spring of 1941 that he had for "many years" nourished the hope of an alliance with Germany was palpably false and insincere. When he confided in me in November of 1938 he thought the then tendency in Japan toward an alignment with Germany and Italy was a profound mistake, and he termed the Japanese militarists who favored such an alignment "damned sword-rattling chauvinists." He hoped that a partnership with the United States would serve as an efficient curb on those militarists for whom he later became an all too willing tool and mouthpiece.

Why his proposals were not even taken seriously in

Washington I do not know. Probably the President and Secretary Hull felt that there was no use in relying on the word or promises of any Japanese leader. And in the light of subsequent events and of many evidences of Japan's faithlessness, this was doubtless a wise decision.

My letter containing the Matsuoka proposals relative to eastern Siberia was duly handed to President Roosevelt, who kept it four days and then returned it to Mr. Sulzberger without comment. Evidently the President chose to reply through official channels, for the letter Mr. Sulzberger sent to me by a roundabout circuit through Hongkong was entirely non-committal, but I have reason to believe that Matsuoka later heard from the White House through Joseph Clark Grew, then the American ambassador to Japan.

Matsuoka, now living in retirement at a small country estate northwest of Tokyo, must be watching the war with alternations of flaming exultation and bitter misgivings. The battles of Manila, Singapore, and Java must have brought him delight, but the Coral Sea and Midway clashes must have aroused doubts and anxieties in his mind. And while he waits and watches, he is certainly planning a return to public life and already devising schemes by which he will attempt to rob the United Nations of the security from future aggressions which is one of their main war aims.

CHAPTER XVIII

Konoye the Gambler

Another of Japan's statesman-politicians being kept in reserve to help negotiate a compromise peace is Prince Fumimaro Konoye, three times Prime Minister and one of the most unstable and unreliable of all the Japanese leaders. His past has been so checkered by various and varying affiliations and his retirement to private life a few months before the attack on Pearl Harbor was so well timed that the Japanese will push him forward as a "patriotic liberal" when they have been defeated and begin trying to squirm out of the necessity of meeting the dictated terms which the United Nations will present for their acceptance.

America and Europe have never assessed Prince Konoye's power and position correctly. He has been a mysterious figure and has served the Army well. His lineage is almost equal to that of the imperial family, and, while his wealth

is not great, he was for years regarded as "the coming man"
of Japanese political life.

All parties and factions courted Konoye, seeking his co-
operation or open allegiance, and the impression spread
abroad that he was an anti-militaristic liberal. Actually,
however, as early as 1935 he made a secret agreement with
the military faction and from then on was regarded by the
war clique as their "ace in the hole," as a powerful Japanese general told me in Mukden one day in 1936.

When Prince Konoye became Premier for the first time
in the early summer of 1937, the New York *Times* cabled
to me in Shanghai to send by mail a 1,500-word article on
how the elevation of this nobleman to the post of Prime
Minister was likely to influence Japan's relations with
China. I sent along an article stating flatly that all ideas that
Konoye was a peace-loving liberal were erroneous, that his
elevation to the head of the Government meant that the
expansionists of the military clique were ready to attack
China, and that hostilities would certainly be precipitated
before autumn.

This article, directly at variance with most of the articles and editorials which greeted Konoye's assumption of
power, was published in the New York *Times* late in June
of 1937. That particular issue of the *Times* made good reading when I came across it in the Tientsin Club late in July,
at just the time when Japanese airplanes were bombarding
the city and reducing Nantao University to a heap of smol-

dering rubble. The Japanese had started the action less than three weeks before by attacking the Chinese at Marco Polo Bridge, on the outskirts of Peiping, on the night of July 7.

Prince Konoye has a curious personality and is singularly lacking in will power and driving force, but like many weak and vacillating men he is tremendously stubborn at unexpected times. Time and again during his three terms as Premier he contracted a "diplomatic illness" as an excuse for going into retirement, and thus managed to permit violent partisan cliques within the Army and Navy to fight out their differences. When the tide toward victory became discernible, the Prince would recover with remarkable alacrity and announce a decision, and an adherence to what was obviously to be the winning side.

Konoye is not robust and frequently suffers from colds and light attacks resembling influenza. Whenever it was announced that the Prime Minister was suffering from a new attack and was inaccessible to callers, conjecture would run wild in Tokyo—was he really ill or was there a new Cabinet crisis pending?

Although as a rule Konoye was willing to be the tool of the most radical wing of the military clique, his character is such that he was often subject to qualms, and at least twice he secretly sought to end the war in China by compromise. On one of these two occasions he attempted to use me as one of his secret emissaries to General Chiang Kai-shek, and at that time he was not only willing but frantically eager to betray the very Army clique which had put him in power and maintained him there.

The Japanese thought they had won the war when they captured Nanking in December of 1937. So certain were they that Chinese resistance had been broken and that Chinese unity would collapse that they needlessly prolonged the period given to resting and reorganizing their tired forces after the victorious campaign which had resulted in storming China's capital.

Meanwhile General Chiang Kai-shek, who had established a new seat of government for China at Hankow, worked tirelessly at reorganizing his own forces and at importing war supplies into central China through Canton and Hongkong, from where they were hauled inland over the Canton-Hankow Railway.

By early summer it became evident that the Japanese were about to launch a new drive up the Yangtsze River with the object of destroying the Chinese armies and capturing Hankow. Soon their armies were fighting their way overland, while the Japanese Navy and Air Force began assaulting the various forts and booms which blocked a direct advance inland by way of the Yangtsze River. They captured Anking; they captured Kiukiang; and China's refugee capital was soon in peril.

It was at this point in the campaign, on October 13, 1938, that there called at my office a Japanese named Bunshiro Suzuki. Mr. Suzuki is little known in the United States, although he has traveled here and in Europe. But in Japan he is a prominent citizen, a large shareholder in several Tokyo and Osaka Japanese-language newspapers, and a writer and commentator of note.

For half an hour Mr. Suzuki talked with amazing frankness about the cost and progress of the Japanese campaigns in China, about the greed and corruption of his Empire's militarists, and about the brutal and bungling manner in which they continued to alienate all Chinese of any standing by denying them even the right of self-respect. I thought he had probably come as a secret agent of that very military group whom he denounced and was bent on sounding out my personal views, so my replies were guarded. At length I told Suzuki that I regretted having to excuse myself, but that I had to keep an important appointment and must bring the interview to an end.

He became flustered. "But I have an urgent and very confidential matter to discuss with you," he blurted out at last. "I have come as the personal emissary of Prince Konoye, and here," producing a packet of papers from inside his shirt front, "are my credentials in both English and Japanese."

"What is this all about? What is your mission?" I asked, and then Suzuki astounded me by this declaration:

"The Prime Minister wants to stop the war. He says the capture of Hankow would be nothing more than military masturbation, and wants to make peace without the Army's knowledge before China's new capital falls."

Suzuki would say nothing more than that, insisting that he must have at least two hours alone with me in order to unfold his plans in detail. We arranged to meet at my home after dinner that evening, and he urged that in the interval I should assure myself of the validity of his credentials by showing them to Mr. Tani, then Japan's ambassador at large in China, or to the Japanese consul general. I did both, and found that the letter in Japanese was in Konoye's own hand, stating that Suzuki enjoyed his complete confidence and carried a verbal message to me of "supreme importance."

At that time—October 1938—much of the world was still marveling at what was called the new technique of diplomacy—namely, Chamberlain's trip by air to Munich to win "peace in our time" by conferring with Hitler. When Mr. Suzuki came to my apartment that evening he amazed me by first declaring that the Chamberlain idea was at least a year old and that Prince Konoye had proposed to fly to Nanking more than a year before in order personally to arrange a Sino-Japanese agreement with General Chiang Kai-shek.

In a letter which I wrote to General Chiang the next day, October 14, I find these paragraphs of direct quotation from Bunshiro Suzuki:

A year ago last July, when the first clash occurred near Peiping, I went to Mr. Hirota (then Foreign Minister), who has long been my close personal friend, and proposed to him exactly what Mr. Chamberlain did last month. In other words, I urged Mr. Hirota to cable to General Chiang Kai-shek and express his willingness to fly to Nanking for a personal conference, at which an attempt would be made to settle all Sino-Japanese differences.

Mr. Hirota welcomed this proposal and discussed the matter with Prince Konoye. The Premier, too, thought well of the proposal, but suggested that he himself should make the flight. The matter was then discussed at length at a secret meeting of the civilian members of the Cabinet, but was voted down on the grounds that Japan would "lose too much face" by seeming to compromise.

Here was evidence of Prince Konoye's first attempt to change policy and betray the military clique which had put him into power to be their instrument and Premier during what they confidently believed would be the quick conquest of China. Having acquiesced in starting hostilities at Marco Polo Bridge, the Prime Minister became faint-hearted and uncertain of the wisdom of the step to which he had helped commit the Empire, and was eager to fly to Nanking to negotiate a durable peace with General Chiang Kai-shek. Presumably some of the civilian members of the Cabinet relayed his intentions to the Ministers of War and Navy, and they succeeded in blocking this Asiatic counterpart of the attempt to assure "peace in our time."

Konoye's second move to betray the militarists who had made him was, in its inspiration, as melodramatic as a motion-picture international spy drama. Here is the plan in detail, in the words of Bunshiro Suzuki, as I wrote them down in my notes that night of October 13 after he had said good-by.

Prince Konoye knows that you are a friend of the generalissimo and believes that he will give serious consideration to any proposal which you guarantee as valid. You have checked on my credentials, and now it is my desire that you accompany me to Hankow and sponsor me while I present to Chiang Kai-shek official credentials from our Premier and a document containing Japan's proposals for a peace with China. The Premier wants to check the Army in its·career of conquest before it becomes an all-powerful threat to the existence of government in Japan.

He fears that if the Army captures Hankow, and China is conquered, Japan itself will come under a naked Army dictatorship, and this he fears will mean the ultimate ruin of the Empire, for having conquered China our militarists would challenge the United States and all positions of the European powers in the Far East. He wants to avoid this at all costs. The people of Japan are tired of this war, and if Prince Konoye could suddenly announce a reasonable peace agreement the Army would not dare to prolong the senseless struggle.

At this point I interrupted to call Mr. Suzuki's attention to the fact that all communication between Shanghai and Hankow was cut off, except by way of Hongkong. How, I asked, was I to get word of Konoye's advances to General

Chiang, and how could he and I make the journey to Hankow if the generalissimo was willing to receive us?

At that time all railways leading into the interior of China, except the Canton-Hankow line, had been disrupted by the war, and fighting on both banks of the Yangtsze, in addition to the Japanese Navy's activities on that great stream, made river traffic an impossibility. I pointed out to Suzuki that the mere transmission of his original proposals presented difficulties because the mails by way of Hongkong and Canton were slow and uncertain, and telegraph and radio communication between Shanghai and Hankow was either ruined or entirely in the hands of Japanese censors.

If the proposal were cabled to Hongkong and then sent to Hankow by land telegraph, there would be little hope of guarding the secrecy of the move, for the Japanese had agents and spies everywhere and were supposed to be in possession of most of the codes in use—even the several secret codes of the American Navy and diplomatic missions in the Far East.

But these difficulties, it seemed, had been considered in advance in Tokyo, for Suzuki replied:

If the generalissimo will receive me, I propose that you and I fly together to Hankow or to any other place he may designate. Prince Konoye will arrange for us to go in a civilian plane of the Shanghai-Peiping line, to be furnished by the Japanese Government. If the generalissimo distrusts these arrangements, he may send any neutral pilot and crew of his own—say American fliers—to take us inland. The plane can have any markings he suggests, so that it will be able to fly over the Chinese lines and land on a Chinese airfield without being fired upon.

For my part, I am willing to be blindfolded during the flight and during my entire stay in Hankow except for such time as I am in the generalissimo's presence. I would, of course, expect no liberty of movement while there. We had planned that the plane would start ostensibly for Peiping and then, when away from Japanese observers, swing westward and make for Hankow. We could probably get such a start that we'd be able to outdistance pursuit if Japanese Army observers or listeners detected the change in our route and sent pursuit planes after us.

If this plan is not approved, I am willing to go to Hongkong with you by an American ship and to fly from Hongkong to Hankow by a British or Chinese plane—just as the generalissimo prefers.

I told Suzuki that the flight arrangements seemed satisfactory, but the greater and initial difficulty would be in getting the proposals for a peace parley to General Chiang. I pointed out that the Japanese forces were advancing up-river rapidly, that the Chinese lines showed signs of crumbling in several sectors, and that it would require at least a week and possibly ten days to get a letter to Hankow by way of Hongkong and Canton. But Suzuki had an answer ready for this objection, too.

We have at least six weeks. Our Army cannot capture Hankow before late November. Admiral Yarnell is in Shanghai. His flagship, the *Augusta*, is in the river here, and must be in hourly wireless communication with the American gunboat at Hankow. The New York *Times* has a man in Hankow. Wouldn't Admiral Yarnell send this proposal, in secret code, to your *Times* man, for personal transmission to the generalissimo?

Then I told Mr. Suzuki that I would not feel free to take a hand in these negotiations without the knowledge and consent of the New York *Times*. A ship was leaving for Hongkong next morning, and I agreed to get a letter aboard addressed to our Hongkong correspondent, asking him to file a cable to the *Times* managing editor which I would enclose.

The *Times* agreed to my participation in the project, but Admiral Harry E. Yarnell, then commander in chief of our Asiatic Fleet, refused to permit his ships to transmit the necessary messages by wireless. One reason was that he believed the Japanese Army had his codes and would take retaliatory action if his flagship transmitted peace proposals without their knowledge. Such retaliatory action might have resulted in war between Japan and the United States.

Early the next morning I was closeted with Admiral Yarnell in his quarters aboard his flagship and put the whole of Konoye's proposals before him. He cited various reasons why it would be a great impropriety for him to sanction the use of the American naval radio for purposes of this kind, but at last reluctantly said that if I could get the proposals to the New York *Times* man in Hankow by mail via Hongkong, he would permit the American gunboat at Hankow to wireless to him, for transmission to me, a one-word message. That word was to be either "Accepted" or "Declined," and either of those words would let Suzuki and me know whether General Chiang Kai-shek would consent to receive us and listen to Prince Konoye's peace proposals.

The admiral walked with me to the head of the gang-way, and just as I was about to descend to his barge, which was waiting to take me from the *Augusta*, moored in mid-stream, to The Bund of Shanghai, he put his hand on my shoulder and said in a voice so low that none of the ship's officers standing by could hear him:

"Abend, I wish you wouldn't attempt this flight. I know it would be a thrilling adventure and might get you the scoop of the year, but the chances are 99 to 100 that the Japanese Army will learn of the venture in advance, and then your plane will be shot down before it gets a hundred miles away from Shanghai. Or you'll be shot when you get back here. Think it over."

My letter to Hankow went to Hongkong by ship, arriving at the British port the morning of October 17. It was flown to Hankow on the eighteenth, and the New York *Times* man in Hankow, knowing nothing of the contents of the sealed enclosure, presented the Konoye proposals to General Chiang Kai-shek in the presence of Madame Chiang the next day. On October 20 came the one-word reply, relayed to me by telephone by Admiral Yarnell. It was, "Accepted."

Immediately I got in touch with Mr. Suzuki, who sailed for Japan that evening to obtain official credentials from the Premier and Konoye's secret terms for a compromise.

But the move for peace had been started too late. On October 25 the Chinese lines defending Hankow broke, and by the evening of the twenty-sixth Japanese forces had occupied the three neighboring Yangtsze cities of Hankow, Wuchang, and Hanyang. General Chiang Kai-shek, his Government, and most of his generals had either flown to Chungking to establish a new Chinese capital or were bound upriver in suffocatingly overcrowded ships which proceeded under a rain of bombs from Japanese planes.

Prince Konoye lacked the determination and vigor to be a wartime Premier, so the Army pushed him out and installed General Tojo at the head of the Government a few months before Pearl Harbor. It is true that Konoye and his Foreign Minister, Yosuke Matsuoka, willingly engineered Japan into formally joining the Rome-Berlin Axis, but there their usefulness ended. Obviously, from the Japanese viewpoint, a general on the active list had to be Premier in wartime. Politicians of the Konoye and Matsuoka stripe are of little value during a period of military dictatorship and virtual martial law. But their value as plotters and negotiators may become great when the time comes to make the peace.

Prince Konoye, as a negotiator, would be as slippery and unreliable and as dangerous for American interests in the Far East as would Matsuoka. In office he was not loyal even to the clique that elevated him to the head of the Government; as a peacemaker he would be doubly ready to betray those with whom he was dealing and to repudiate his personal promises and official commitments.

CHAPTER XIX

No Soft Peace!

Nobody really believes that his own home or business will be destroyed by fire, but all prudent people carry fire insurance.

Nations which start wars are usually confident that they will win before the peoples they have attacked can muster their full strength. But prudent nations like to arrange for insurance against a possible defeat, and the best form of such insurance is to launch in the lands of their enemies subtle propaganda campaigns aimed at securing a soft peace.

History may or may not repeat itself, but propaganda certainly does. In 1917 and 1918 the American people listened to clever propaganda to the effect that we were not fighting Germany, that our only real enemies were "the wicked Kaiser and his militarists." We gave heed to that propaganda, won the war, and lost the peace. That is one of the main reasons we are in our present plight.

The same sort of propaganda against possible defeat is being carried on in this country today by both Japan and Germany. Month after month it increases in volume and broadens its appeal. More and more voices are being raised, more and more books and articles are being written to convince the American people that we are not fighting Japan, but that it is only "the wicked Japanese war lords" and the "hotheaded younger officers group" who were responsible for the attack on Pearl Harbor. And from Berlin a similar propaganda is being directed: this time, we are told, we are not fighting the German people, but only "Hitler and his wicked Nazi leaders."

The avowedly anti-Christian Nazis and the proudly un-Christian Japanese propaganda workers are so unscrupulous that they are making an increasing use of the Bible. The mails these days carry an astonishing amount of semi-religious propaganda reminding that the Holy Writ counsels us to love our enemies, to be merciful to vanquished foes, and to cleanse our hearts of hatred and leave vengeance to the Most High.

Paid propaganda agents of our enemies are working not only in the great cities, but in the rural districts and in portions of this country where population is sparse. One of these well-paid propaganda agents, now interned for the duration, was arrested in a little Vermont town with a population of only 788 people.

This brings us to the case of the Rev. Yutaka Minakuchi

Born in Japan, Minakuchi came to this country as a boy of fourteen in 1897. He has lived here continuously for nearly forty-five years, except for a three-month period in 1938 when he made a trip to Japan, China, and Manchuria. At the turn of the century he received an excellent education, attending four of our great universities—Virginia, South Carolina, Transylvania, and Yale. Later he went to the graduate school at Oberlin, received a degree in theology, and in 1910 was ordained as a Congregational minister.

For a time Minakuchi was pastor of a church in Chesterfield, Illinois. Then he became a Chautauqua lecturer, and during World War I he campaigned through the middle western states for the Liberty Bond and Red Cross drives. In 1921 he met and married an American girl born and raised in Glover, Vermont. They settled in Glover, where their two daughters were born. In 1927 Minakuchi became pastor of a church at Peacham, Vermont, and remained there until 1938. Then he returned to Glover and acted as a supply preacher until after December 7, when he was registered as an enemy alien.

About a month after the attack on Pearl Harbor I read with distrust a two-column interview with Minakuchi which appeared in the Burlington *Free Press*. Here are some of the main points in that interview:

The people of Japan did not want this war. They were forced into it by a small military clique which has taken over control of the Government.

The Pearl Harbor attack must have been carried out by some of the young hotheads who are part of the military machine which is in control of the Government.

It is not true that the Japanese are naturally a militaristic race.

Months before the outbreak of the war in the Pacific this Minakuchi was working slyly to influence opinion in favor of having the United States attempt the role of mediator between Japan and China. In an article he wrote for the Orleans County *Monitor*, he said:

Many are the lovers of peace and some of them are capable of Christian thinking. From them have come numerous protests against Japan's course of action in China. I do not doubt their motives being sincere and well-meaning. I am, however, keenly disappointed in the absence of any appeal for reconciliation between China and Japan, and much less any friendly efforts on the part of the peace-lovers towards bridging the chasm which keeps the two great nations apart.

Granting that Japan is aggressive and that China is passive, siding with China against Japan will not give a harmony to East Asia out of which a nobler life should come forth. They may be divided now, but they are the indispensable links in a chain and each has a great mission to fulfill.

Why can't America, who has never entertained any territorial ambition on the Asiatic continent, be the champion of conciliation in international incidents? Let America say to China and Japan something like this: "We are hoping to build on this western continent a better and safer community without walls and without armaments, where races and peoples may live on the basis of mutual helpfulness. You, too, may do likewise in East Asia knowing that you are neighbors and that you are of the same blood and culture as well."

Inquiry developed the fact that when he returned from Japan in 1938 Minakuchi talked and preached in defense of Japan's expansionist policy at the expense of China and formulated a Fascistlike philosophy.

All of this sounded ominous, so I wrote a letter to the editor of the Burlington *Free Press* and asked him to publish it. In my letter I pointed out that Minakuchi's arguments were being used far and wide in this country by enemy propagandists.

This brought a storm of criticism. My mail was filled with letters condemning me for criticizing a minister and a "defenseless foreigner." One letter published in the *Free Press* was written by the pastor of a church at Fairfax, Vermont, called me a "self-appointed witch hunter," and broadly hinted that I was probably "the paid or unpaid advocate working on behalf of the 1,000 millionaire jingoists made during the last war."

Soon this unimportant local storm died down. But two months later the Rev. Yutaka Minakuchi was arrested on a Presidential warrant charging him with being an enemy alien dangerous to the peace and security of the United States. Arthur Cornelius, FBI agent in charge of the case, announced that for many years Minakuchi had been receiving $250 regularly every month from the Japanese consul general at New York and that he drew this pay as a propaganda agent of the Japanese Imperial Government.

Minakuchi's pay as a propagandist was about twice as much as the salary he earned as a preacher in a Vermont village. In his Vermont home, when the federal agents seized Minakuchi's files, correspondence, ledgers, and diaries, they also found a costly short-wave radio, a camera, and a large supply of films—items banned from alien possession by Presidential proclamation.

Propaganda of the brand that Minakuchi specialized in is not only a form of insurance against Japan's defeat, but also a method of "softening up" the American people so that we will be willing to make a soft peace. It runs directly counter to the war aims of the United Nations, as embodied in the Atlantic Charter framed in the summer of 1941 by President Roosevelt and Premier Churchill when they met at sea.

That Atlantic Charter promises all nations, victors and vanquished, fair and just access to the world's war materials, promises all peoples who have been subjugated by force the right of determining their own political futures, and also declares that all aggressor nations and potential aggressors must be disarmed. That is as "soft" a peace as we dare to permit at the end of this war. Any "softer" terms would mean that once more we had won the war and lost the peace and that Japan and Germany would try their luck again in another fifteen or twenty years.

For a decade the American people and the American Government have been fooled by this kind of propaganda about Japan. When the Japanese began grabbing Manchuria in 1931, we were told not to make any harsh move; "let the financiers and the intellectuals and the liberals have a chance to get the upper hand and kick out the militarists." Well, we gave them ten years, those supposed "liberals" of Japan. And at the end of ten years we had to dig trenches near Pearl Harbor in which to bury more than 2,800 of our sailor and soldier dead.

This is not a war against "the Japanese war lords." It is a war against Japan, the nation, the race. For half a century they have lived and expanded by conquest and loot—the loot from each conquest being used to finance the next war of expansion.

The Minakuchi case is not vitally important in itself, but it is of immense importance as evidence that no community is too small for this kind of softening propaganda to be considered well worth the money that it costs. It is of immense importance as evidence that our enemies do not hesitate to use even our ministers and our churches to spread their propaganda for a "soft" peace. And it shows clearly that if we are not eternally on the alert we may win the war only to lose the peace—again.

CHAPTER XX

The Mist of Words

THE URGE to nationalism and freedom and the hatred of imperialism felt by hundreds of millions of Asiatics could be turned into a gigantic asset for the United Nations if a specific postwar program for Asia were to be announced at once. The Atlantic Charter, sweeping as are some of its declarations, does not suffice. What is urgently needed is a Pacific Charter.

Victory in this war depends fully as much on support of the world's masses as it does on mass production of airplanes and tanks. Already we have been silent for too long, and as a result of this silence some of the peoples of East Asia are losing faith in our integrity. They begin to suspect that we are fighting for a modified form of empire and that in the case of victory we shall grant only such concessions to the yellow men and the brown as we dare not withhold.

Japanese propaganda to the effect that this is a racial war, a color war, is partly responsible for this deplorable development. But the continued reluctance to make a clear enunciation of aims and intentions has assisted the spread and acceptance of Japanese propaganda, in spite of the fact that China, the greatest of Asiatic nations, is firmly anti-Axis.

We should end all doubts and misgivings, voice our intentions with unmistakable clarity, and co-operate in every way possible with the politically conscious groups in all lands now occupied by the Japanese forces. Constant reiteration of our intentions by radio, by smuggled documents, by leaflets dropped from our airplanes, and by word of mouth taken to captive peoples by workers who dare to penetrate into enemy-held territory will result in a spread of sabotage and guerrilla warfare that will seriously sap the strength of Japan. Properly proclaimed war aims, promises of equality of treatment for hitherto suppressed or backward peoples, will release a latent dynamism in areas where there is now either hopelessness, indifference, or actual distrust. There must be understanding, harmony of purpose, and mutual confidence.

Already millions of Chinese and other Asiatics have given their lives for freedom in this long war in which we are new participants. The freedom-loving Asiatics cannot win the war without our help, and we cannot win the war without their help. If we win the war with their assistance and then disappoint them in fashioning the postwar world, we shall know no enduring peace. Now is the time to clarify these issues and begin a co-operation for known and agreed ends.

The United States must take the lead in this vital matter. Britain is suspect and even hated in India and elsewhere in Asia; the Netherlands is an interested party; and no other one of the United Nations is well enough known in the Far East to be listened to attentively. Indeed no other one of those nations is powerful enough to induce imperialism to relinquish its claims upon Asiatic peoples or to force such a relinquishment if force becomes necessary.

It may seem impolitic openly to discuss the possible use of threats or of force among allies, but if any one of the interested powers should insist upon eventually restoring prewar colonial conditions in East Asia or should refuse to agree to a generous Pacific Charter, the United States, which is financing and helping to arm half the world today, would probably have to do no more than issue a reminder of this fact to secure acquiescence. No nation with selfish interests should be permitted to deprive the United Nations of the support and co-operation of the peoples of Asia by clinging to ancient "rights" or by insisting on the perpetuation of ancient wrongs.

In some quarters it is argued that it is an unpropitious time to announce postwar plans when our ships are still being sunk by enemy submarines and when the tide of battle may still go against us on half a dozen vital fronts. In other quarters it is argued that our whole attention should be centered on how to win the war and that it would be folly to "waste time" thinking about the peace.

Unity and increased co-operation will help to win the war, and the assurances of a just peace will bring an increase of support to the United Nations cause. Nothing so quickly brings about a dry rot of morale as skepticism about ultimate aims, and unhappily such skepticism is already abroad in the world today.

Uncounted columns of words have been issued about war aims and peace intentions. In fact our war aims and peace intentions have been obscured by a very mist of words. Pronouncements of good intentions, vague promises, ambiguous pledges that may or may not apply in specific cases —these have so befogged the great issues that clarification is urgently needed.

President Roosevelt has made a greater number of specific statements and pledges than has the head of any other of the United Nations. But only where the Atlantic Charter is concerned have Premier Churchill and Queen Wilhelmina and the heads of the other United Nations definitely promised to uphold any of these pledges. Secretary of State Hull and Under Secretary Welles have also announced aims and intentions which have earned no repetition from the foreign offices of other countries.

The waiting world of today well remembers that a quarter of a century ago another American president made promises to a world at war and that these promises were later repudiated by the United States. What assurance is there, it is asked, that the "four freedoms" and other promises—even the Atlantic Charter itself—may not finally meet the fate of Woodrow Wilson's Fourteen Points and other declarations of intention?

Regardless of who may be our allies during the war, it seems somewhat problematical as to who will be our allies at the making of the peace after a United Nations victory.

In spite of the promises of the Atlantic Charter, Premier Churchill in November 1942 made it plain in a speech in London that he had not accepted the Prime Minister's portfolio in order to preside at the dismembering of the British Empire.

This statement, significantly, followed the announcement in the House of Commons by Richard Kidston Law, Parliamentary Under Secretary for Foreign Affairs, to the effect that Britain has no intention whatsoever of surrendering Hongkong to China after the war's end.

The situation as regards abolishing imperialism and carrying out the Atlantic Charter pledge concerning giving all peoples the right to choose the government under which they shall live has been further complicated by the declaration of Brigadier-General Lord Croft, who, as Joint Parliamentary Under Secretary for the British War Office, said to the House of Commons: "We intend to drive out the aggressor from Malaya and Burma, and restore happiness and liberty to those unhappy countries. Far from quitting, we have the opportunity of continuing to lift those countries from illiteracy to understanding, and some day, in our own wisdom and at our own time, into full self-expression, and, by our example, lead the world to a fuller, happier life."

Are American expeditionary forces in the Orient, then, expected to fight to restore British imperialism?

In black-and-white contrast to these British pronouncements was the incisive statement of war aims made by Joseph Stalin when he spoke at the ceremonies celebrating Soviet Russia's twenty-fifth anniversary of existence. Said he:

The program of action of the Anglo-Soviet-American coalition is: abolition of racial exclusiveness, equality of nations and integrity of their territories, liberation of enslaved nations and restoration of their sovereign rights, the right of every nation to arrange its affairs as it wishes, economic aid to nations which have suffered, and assistance to them in attaining their material welfare, restoration of democratic liberties, the destruction of the Hitlerite regime.

These utterances seem to put the United States and Soviet Russia on the same platform, advocating not only the carrying out of the pledges of the Atlantic Charter but also the promises of the "four freedoms." Opposed to them stand at least the Tory spokesmen of the British Empire, if not Britain itself. The implications are grave.

It is doubtful if ever since the days of the ancient tyrannies any nation has been secretly committed to such sweeping pledges and duties as those to which President Roosevelt committed the United States when, in August of 1941, he sailed away on what was supposed to be a much-needed vacation and fishing trip. Meeting Churchill in Placentia Bay, Newfoundland, he and the British Premier framed the Atlantic Charter, signed it, and then announced it to a startled world.

This document committed the United States and the British Empire to the carrying out of a world revolution, social and economic, in addition to pledging all the resources of both countries to the defeat of the Axis. Although the American public did not recognize the fact at the time the Atlantic Charter was made public, it was virtually a joint declaration of war against Japan, for the eighth point, providing for the disarmament of aggressor nations, made a long continuance of peace in the Pacific impossible.

Here is the official joint announcement of the signing of the Atlantic Charter, as issued in Washington and in London on August 14, 1941:

The President of the United States and the Prime Minister, Mr. Churchill, representing His Majesty's Government in the United Kingdom, have met at sea.

They have been accompanied by officials of their two governments, including high-ranking officers of their military, naval, and air services.

The Mist of Words 285

The whole problem of the supply of munitions of war, as provided by the Lease-Lend Act, for the armed forces of the United States and for those countries actively engaged in resisting aggression has been further examined. Lord Beaverbrook, the Minister of Supply of the British Government, has joined in these conferences. He is going to proceed to Washington to discuss further details with appropriate officials of the United States Government. These conferences will also cover the supply problems of the Soviet Union.

The President and the Prime Minister have had several conferences. They have considered the dangers to world civilization arising from the policies of military domination by conquest upon which the Hitlerite government of Germany and other governments associated therewith have embarked, and have made clear the steps which their countries are respectively taking for their safety in the face of these dangers.

JOINT DECLARATION

They have agreed upon the following joint declaration:

The President of the United States of America and the Prime Minister, Mr. Churchill, representing His Majesty's Government in the United Kingdom, being met together, deem it right to make certain common principles in the national policies of their respective countries on which they base their hopes for a better future for the world.

First: Their countries seek no aggrandizement, territorial or other;

Second: They desire to see no territorial changes that do not accord with the freely expressed wishes of the people concerned;

Third: They respect the right of all peoples to choose the form of government under which they will live; and they wish to see sovereign rights and self-government restored to those who have been forcibly deprived of them;

Fourth: They will endeavor, with due respect for their existing obligations, to further the enjoyment by all states, great or small, victor or vanquished, of access, on equal terms, to the trade and to the raw materials of the world which are needed for their economic prosperity;

Fifth: They desire to bring about the fullest collaboration between all nations in the economic field, with the object of securing, for all, improved labor standards, economic adjustment, and social security;

Sixth: After the final destruction of the Nazi tyranny, they hope to see established a peace which will afford to all nations the means of dwelling in safety within their own boundaries, and which will afford assurance that all the men in all the lands may live out their lives in freedom from fear and want;

Seventh: Such a peace should enable all men to traverse the high seas and oceans without hindrance;

Eighth: They believe that all of the nations of the world, for realistic as well as spiritual reasons, must come to the abandonment of the use of force. Since no future peace can be maintained if land, sea, or air armaments continue to be employed by nations which threaten, or may threaten, aggression outside of their frontiers, they believe, pending the establishment of a wider and permanent system of general security, that the disarmament of such nations is essential. They will likewise aid and encourage all other practicable measures which will lighten for peace-loving peoples the crushing burden of armaments.

FRANKLIN D. ROOSEVELT
WINSTON S. CHURCHILL

One year later, August 14, 1942, President Roosevelt, noting the first anniversary of the signing of the Atlantic Charter, cabled a message to Churchill. The President's cable closed with these words: "We reaffirm our principles. They will bring us to a happier world."

If any reaffirmation of the Atlantic Charter was ever cabled to this country by Churchill, Washington made no announcement of that fact. London newspapers, though they gave prominent display to Roosevelt's anniversary announcement, published nothing similar from any official British source.

The Atlantic Charter remains the only officially adopted pronouncement of the war aims of the United Nations. On January 2, 1942, the heads or official representatives of twenty-six nations issued the following joint text at Washington:

DECLARATION BY UNITED NATIONS

A joint declaration by the United States of America, the United Kingdom of Great Britain and Northern Ireland, and the Union of Soviet Socialist Republics, China, Australia, Belgium, Canada, Costa Rica, Cuba, Czecho-Slovakia, Dominican

Republic, El Salvador, Greece, Guatemala, Haiti, Honduras, India, Luxembourg, Netherlands, New Zealand, Nicaragua, Norway, Panama, Poland, South Africa, Yugoslavia.

The governments signatory hereto,

Having subscribed to a common program of purposes and principles embodied in the joint declaration of the President of the United States of America and the Prime Minister of the United Kingdom of Great Britain and Northern Ireland dated Aug. 14, 1941, known as the Atlantic Charter, being convinced that complete victory over their enemies is essential to defend life, liberty, independence, and religious freedom, and to preserve human rights and justice in their own lands as well as in other lands, and that they are now engaged in a common struggle against savage and brutal forces seeking to subjugate the world, declare:

(1) Each government pledges itself to employ its full resources, military or economic, against those members of the Tripartite Pact and its adherents with which such government is at war.

(2) Each government pledges itself to co-operate with the governments signatory hereto and not to make a separate armistice or peace with the enemies.

The foregoing declaration may be adhered to by other nations.

In the interval between January 2 and November 1 six other nations or refugee governments declared war against the Axis and signed the United Nations declaration. These are: Brazil, Ecuador, Ethiopia, Fighting France, Mexico, and the Philippine Commonwealth, bringing the total to thirty-two.

President Roosevelt's famous "four freedoms" are also generally accepted as among the main war aims of the United Nations. As a matter of record, however, these four freedoms were defined in a message to Congress on January 6, 1941, nearly a year before we were at war. Portions of this message said:

"We are committed to the full support of all those resolute peoples, everywhere, who are resisting aggression. . . .

"We are committed to the proposition that principles of morality and considerations for our own security will never permit us to acquiesce in a peace dictated by aggressors and sponsored by appeasers."

Further outlining conditions of a peace which might be acceptable to the United States, the message listed the following four as indispensable:

1. Freedom of speech and expression—everywhere in the world.

2. Freedom of religious worship—everywhere in the world.

3. Freedom from want, through economic understanding—everywhere in the world.

4. Freedom from fear, through world-wide reduction of armaments—everywhere in the world.

These are brave words, but still only words. And words have long been the currency of diplomacy. Like other currencies, they have all too often been subject to inflation and thereby lost value, and many a time they have been subject to actual repudiation.

On July 23, 1942, the American Secretary of State, Cordell Hull, made a radio broadcast from a carefully prepared text which had been approved in advance by President Roosevelt. Some of Secretary Hull's pronouncements on that occasion further obscured the view of ultimate peace aims by limiting promises of freedom to those nations and peoples who had earned the right to receive these precious gifts. One of these specific qualifications was as follows:

We have always believed—and we believe today—that all peoples, without distinction of race, color, or religion, who are prepared and willing to accept the responsibilities of liberty are entitled to its enjoyment.

We have always sought—and we seek today—to encourage and aid all who aspire to freedom to establish their right to it by preparing themselves to assume its obligations. . . .

It has been our purpose in the past—and will remain our purpose in the future—to use the full measure of our influence to support attainment of freedom by all peoples who, by their acts, show themselves worthy of it and ready for it. . . .

In many quarters this portion of Secretary Hull's broadcast was interpreted as a warning to India, but if it was meant as such Gandhi merely shrugged his shoulders and paid no heed.

The following paragraphs were thought to have been intended for reading particularly in Vichy:

All these advances—in political freedom, in economic betterment, in social justice, in spiritual values—can be achieved by each nation primarily through its own work and effort, mainly through its own wise policies and actions. They can be made only where there is acceptance and cultivation of the concepts and the spirit of human rights and human freedom.

It is impossible for any nation or group of nations to prescribe the methods or provide the means by which any other nation can accomplish or maintain its own political and economic independence, be strong, prosper, and attain high spiritual goals. It is possible, however, for all nations to give and to receive help.

If this subtle warning was meant for the Pétain-Laval clique in France, it was strangely contradicted by Under Secretary Welles when he told the Vichy ambassador at Washington that "the Government of the United States fervently hopes that it may see the re-establishment of the independence of France and of the integrity of French territory."

This communication was taken to mean that the United States favors the complete restoration of the French colonial system, which would mean handing Indo-China back to France after the war. What encouragement could the millions of native peoples of Asia draw from a pronouncement of this kind?

And yet, if this was the original intention, there was a quick change of policy, for about six weeks later Mr. Welles, speaking at Arlington, said:

If this war is in fact a war for the liberation of peoples, it must assure the sovereign equality of peoples throughout the world, as well as in the world of the Americas. Our victory must bring in its train the liberation of all peoples. . . . The age of imperialism is ended. The right of a people to their freedom must be recognized. . . . The selfishness of small groups . . . will not be allowed to block the new frontier of human welfare.

Brave words again. But again they have not been subscribed to officially by Great Britain, by the Netherlands, or by any other of the thirty-two countries comprising the United Nations.

Although Secretary Hull in his July broadcast stressed the fact that the all-important issue is the winning of the war, he also stressed the need, as a war measure, for formulating policies for the eventual days of peace. On this point he said:

Without impediment to the fullest prosecution of the war —indeed for its most effective prosecution—the United Nations should from time to time, as they did in adopting the Atlantic Charter, formulate and proclaim their common views regarding fundamental policies which will chart for mankind a wise course based on enduring spiritual values.

In support of such policies, an informed public opinion must be developed. This is a task of intensive study, hard thinking, broad vision, and leadership—not for governments alone, but for parents, and teachers, and clergymen, and all those, within each nation, who provide spiritual, moral, and intellectual guidance. Never did so great and so compelling a duty in this respect devolve upon those who are in positions of responsibility, public and private.

Mr. Welles has been chosen as the administration's spokesman who has tested public opinion on the subject of a very long armistice period to be followed by making peace regionally and at informed leisure, instead of a short armistice and a peace based on guesswork as to the equity of new frontiers and new economic arrangements. So far there has been no opposition, except by newspapers like the Chicago *Tribune,* to the long armistice suggestion.

Certainly in all East Asia, with the single exception of China, the liberated areas must remain under the administration of representatives of the United Nations for varying periods of time, none of which can be short. The victors will have a deep obligation to set up an international control to co-operate with the literate and politically intelligent elements of each native population until such time as a literate electorate can be developed and the peoples can be adequately prepared for self-government.

The British Liberal party in August 1942 based its international policy on Secretary Hull's July 23 broadcast and adopted resolutions declaring that "all colonial possessions throughout the world must come under the general control and protection of an international body. The guiding principles of the controlling authority must be the well-being of the colonial peoples, the 'open door,' the training of natives in the development of free institutions with the object of enabling them progressively to manage their own affairs."

These are formidable tasks indeed. In many huge, thickly populated areas of Asia there is today not one qualified teacher to every twenty thousand illiterates. The mere task of educating and training the teachers who are to educate and train these hundreds of millions of Asiatics who are to be set free is a task of appalling magnitude. And, like scores of other tasks which will require quick doing with the coming of peace, there has as yet been no basic plan for training these teachers. There is even no preparation to teach the necessary languages to the men and women who will have to be the administrators and the teachers of the lands which will look to the United Nations for succor and for training. These vast projects, if they are to be carried to a successful conclusion, will require a continuation of the self-denials and sacrifices to which the war will accustom the peoples of all of the United Nations as it drags into the long future.

Henry A. Wallace, Vice President of the United States, in his widely discussed address on May 8, 1942, before the Free World Association declared:

No nation will have the God-given right to exploit other nations. Older nations will have the privilege to help younger nations get started on the path to industrialization, but there must be neither military nor economic imperialism. . . . Yes, and when the time of peace comes, the citizen will have the duty, the supreme duty, of sacrificing the lesser interests for the greater interest of the general welfare. Those who write the peace must think of the whole world. There can be no privileged peoples.

This brings up again Japan's position in an East Asia where there is to be justice meted out to all peoples. It must be clear that until Japan can learn to be a good neighbor to all nations bordering on the Pacific Ocean she cannot expect complete self-determination. Unless Japan fashions for herself a government which can be counted upon for peaceful co-operation in the maintenance of stability in the Far East, the victors must reserve the right to intervene in Japanese domestic affairs.

Until the Japanese evince a real will to international decency (and this applies also to Germany and to Italy) their country must be one of the underprivileged lands of the world. Vice President Wallace says there can be "no privileged peoples," but certainly the nations which have made colossal sacrifices to end international banditry will, for a time, have the combined privilege and onerous duty of re-establishing international law and order and of directing the rebuilding of a civilization that will be revealed as lying half in ruins when the smoke of the final battle clears away.

Japan must be subjected to no punitive indemnities other than the loss of her investments in lands which she has invaded and conquered and suppressed. She will, however, have to repay individuals and corporations for property stolen and damages sustained by action of her vicious military. But Japan must at once be amply fed. If the victors discriminate against the vanquished in such humanitarian matters as food distribution, medical assistance, and the rebuilding of shattered economies, then the victors will prove themselves as bad as the savageries they will have quelled.

Japan must suffer no discrimination in the matter of quick and free access to the markets and raw materials of neighboring Asia and other parts of the world, and such underprivilege as she must suffer must be limited solely to activities in spheres in which she can again become a danger to the peace of the Pacific. She will, as a matter of course, suffer the underprivilege of being debarred from maintaining the peace of the world, and she will also have to suffer the humiliation of having to accept tutelage in decency just as though she were one of the backward nations unfitted to handle her own affairs.

The vitality of Japan is already seriously sapped. For the first time in many decades civilian deaths alone greatly outnumber births. Even in 1941, before Japan plunged into all-out war, the national standard of living was more than 50 per cent below the 1935–36 standard.

There will be a great and growing campaign against dealing sternly with outlaw nations. Even in the refugee ship *Gripsholm*, which late in August brought nearly fifteen hundred American and other refugees from Japan and other parts of East Asia, meetings were held by some of the American passengers advocating a soft peace. These same American citizens, be it said to their shame, were active in Japan before the outbreak of hostilities, publicly urging a "more cautious" policy on the part of the United States Government and upholding Japan's career of aggression and savage suppression of conquered peoples.

There is a vast difference, which some types of mind fail to grasp, between devotion to humanitarianism and a disloyalty which may amount even to unconscious treason. There are always ready and active clever enemy agents alert to utilize the unthinking and misguided, and during this war—and after this war—one of the insidious ways in which enemy agents will try to save something from the wreckage of total defeat will be to play upon the well-known "Big Brother" impulse of the American people.

As a nation we have for many decades been willing to lead any humanitarian project, to give of our sympathy, our wealth, and our effort to cure distresses existing in any part of the world. Now we must develop vision enough to understand that, unless we are ready as a nation to assume genuine continuous leadership and help prevent the development of these distresses, we shall be lacking in fundamental humanitarianism. But our humanitarianism must not be of so soft and foolish a character that we shall permit the development of another situation which will inevitably lead to another war—and again to new problems of helping the famishing survivors.

On June 2, 1942, Secretary Hull and China's Foreign Minister, T. V. Soong, signed a little-noticed Mutual Aid Agreement which offers the pattern of our economic attitude toward the Far East—Japan included. This Mutual Aid Agreement commits the United States and China to common action "directed to the expansion, by appropriate international and domestic measures, of production, employment, and the exchange and consumption of goods, which are the material foundations of the liberty and welfare of all peoples; to the elimination of all forms of discriminatory treatment in international commerce; to the reduction of tariffs and other trade barriers."

There is no mist of obscurity about this joint declaration. It is the economic declaration of what must be the new Pacific Charter. Unhappily, so far it relates only to the United States and to China, but it must eventually be made universal in application.

On analysis an agreement of this kind is of almost incalculable importance not only to the Chinese but also to the American people. In the Orient, to take food alone, between

70 and 76 per cent of the average family budget goes for food. In this country the proportion is considerably less than 50 per cent. China, Japan, and all East Asia must have a minimum standard of public nutrition; this is now conceded to be an affair of government all over the world. Prices and supplies are now being kept under control by wartime measures and subsidies. If our economic pact with China is a pattern for postwar economy, some similar controls will have to be continued in the postwar world.

The end of the war will find the United States the greatest producer of raw materials and manufactured products that the world has ever known, and it will have the greatest number of skilled workers. In much of the rest of the world there will be ruin and hunger. If it is not possible to finance continuing full-blast production, gradually turning from war material to peace materials, then chaos will develop here too. This production turnover must be accompanied by gradually rising standards of living in all parts of the world—not merely by the relaxation of rationing and wartime restrictions at home and continuing intense want abroad.

Frontiers and sovereignties will have to await delayed discussions. The first problems will be those of transport, food, and fuel. If these problems are not handled efficiently the starving Far East may disintegrate while the victors are still celebrating their triumphs—and in that event the triumphs will be meaningless.

Those who expect anything like a spontaneous world-wide combination for the common good with the coming of peace will be bitterly disappointed. Even among the victors there will be nothing like a reign of universal good will. Instead, there will be clashing claims, greed, and selfishness. Only if the strongest of the victors have, in addition to their power, the will to lead and to act, will there be order and equity in the world. We must adhere to our highest moral purposes, for if we forget our moral obligations to the rest of the world the exercise of power will become intolerable to other nations once the peril of defeat is a thing of the past.

One of the dangers of the immediate postwar period will be that the people of the United States may suffer an extreme distaste for the whole of the Far East—for all foreign countries. Our interest will have been keyed abnormally high for overlong, and there will be a natural tendency to relax and turn in upon ourselves and our own problems. This distaste is certain to be accentuated by the presence in Washington and elsewhere in this country of a legion of propagandists shouting the merits of contradictory claims. Selfish and clamoring claimants for this clique and that faction, this area and that project, are likely to turn our humanitarianism and public-spiritedness into sour cynicism.

That will be precisely the period in which it will be essential to claim and maintain the privileges of our prestige.

We have hitherto been lacking in the psychology of leadership. Being a self-reliant people, we have a tendency to put others on their feet and then tell them to "go it alone." We harshly condemned Britain for Chamberlain's failure to intervene in Europe, and then, later, when Britain was engaged in a desperate struggle for survival, we refused to face the necessity for intervention in the Far East.

After the war Europe's collective power and prestige will be vastly diminished compared with the power and prestige of the United States. In the Orient, China will loom in major importance above the stature in the Far East of any European nation. In Europe our natural partnership will be with Britain and to a lesser extent with Soviet Russia. In the Orient we shall act in concert with the new China instead of largely with Great Britain as we have done in the past. And there will be new ties with Australia and New Zealand, both of which will probably have to look to the United States instead of to Britain for further financing.

This situation will call for a peace settlement of extreme flexibility. New nations will rise to new power; Japan will eventually re-emerge and take her place with the law-abiding nations of the world. If a non-flexible peace settlement is drawn up, making no provisions for gradual and lawful change, then change will be attempted by violence, and such attempts will have to be met with violence. The maps drawn in 1950 will probably be outdated by 1960 unless the workings of the laws of growth and change are obstructed by conservatism.

President Roosevelt struck a high, clear note on January 6, 1942, when in his message to Congress he declared:

I know that I speak for the American people—and I have good reason to believe that I speak also for all the other peoples who fight with us—when I say that this time we are determined not only to win the war but also to maintain the security of the peace which will follow. . . . We are fighting today for security, for progress, and for peace, not only for ourselves but for all men, not only for one generation, but for all generations. We are fighting to cleanse the world of ancient evils, ancient ills.

The American people are now fighting and sacrificing to win a war that they want followed by a just settlement of the world's ills. If we help to frame a just peace which can be maintained only by the proper use of American power, and if we then withdraw again into isolationism and refuse to use that power, all will have gone for nought—even our good intentions. And hell will have a new paving of a magnificence never dreamed of by the fallen angels.